Zero to Python Hero

A Complete Roadmap to Learn Python Fast and Land Your First Tech Job

Booker Blunt

Rafael Sanders

Miguel Farmer

Boozman Richard

How to Scan a Barcode to Get a Repository

1. **Install a QR/Barcode Scanner** – Ensure you have a barcode or QR code scanner app installed on your smartphone or use a built-in scanner in **GitHub, GitLab, or Bitbucket.**

2. **Open the Scanner** – Launch the scanner app and grant necessary camera permissions.

3. **Scan the Barcode** – Align the barcode within the scanning frame. The scanner will automatically detect and process it.

4. **Follow the Link** – The scanned result will display a **URL to the repository**. Tap the link to open it in your web browser or Git client.

5. **Clone the Repository** – Use **Git clone** with the provided URL to download the repository to your local machine.

Chapter 1: Introduction to Python and the Tech Industry

Overview of Python's Role in Tech

Python has quickly become one of the most popular and versatile programming languages used across the globe. Known for its simplicity and readability, Python has found applications in nearly every aspect of the tech industry. It is used for web development, data analysis, artificial intelligence, machine learning, automation, software development, and more. Python's design philosophy emphasizes code readability and simplicity, making it an ideal choice for beginners and professionals alike.

Python is an open-source language, which means it's free to use and constantly evolving with contributions from developers worldwide. The language's simplicity allows programmers to write fewer lines of code, which means faster development time and easier maintenance. Its broad ecosystem of libraries and frameworks, such as Flask and Django for web development, pandas and NumPy for data science, and TensorFlow and scikit-learn for machine learning, has propelled Python to the forefront of modern software development.

In fact, Python is often chosen for cutting-edge applications such as artificial intelligence, data science, automation, and cloud computing, all of which are integral parts of the tech industry today. By learning Python, you're setting yourself up for a career in some of the most dynamic fields in tech.

Why Learn Python?

1. Simplicity and Readability

When it comes to learning a programming language, Python is an excellent choice for newcomers. It's designed to be easy to read, with a clean and straightforward syntax that resembles English. Python allows developers to focus more on solving problems rather than deciphering complex syntax.

For example, Python eliminates the need for brackets and semi-colons, making the code visually simpler and easier to maintain. This simplicity has made Python the go-to language for beginners and even those new to the tech industry.

2. Versatility Across Fields

Python's versatility is one of its most attractive qualities. The language is used in a variety of sectors, from finance and healthcare to entertainment and space exploration. Whether you're interested in web development, data analysis, or building machine learning algorithms, Python can handle it all.

Its rich library support further makes Python adaptable. Popular tools such as TensorFlow (for deep learning) and pandas (for data manipulation) have made Python a dominant force in cutting-edge tech fields.

3. Extensive Community and Resources

Learning Python opens up access to one of the largest and most active programming communities in the world. The Python Software Foundation, along with an extensive network of contributors and enthusiasts, ensures that Python is consistently updated and well-maintained. As a beginner, you'll have access to a wealth of tutorials, documentation, forums, and blogs to guide you on your journey.

Additionally, there are many frameworks and libraries that extend Python's capabilities, making it easier to build complex applications. These resources are available to everyone, from casual hobbyists to professional developers.

4. High Demand for Python Developers

The demand for Python developers is skyrocketing across industries. According to recent industry reports, Python ranks as one of the top programming languages for job openings, and its usage has only grown in recent years. Companies that specialize in machine learning, artificial intelligence, and cloud computing rely heavily on Python for developing their systems. Many of these companies actively seek Python developers to design and maintain sophisticated applications.

By mastering Python, you gain a valuable skill that is in high demand in the job market. Whether you're interested in joining a tech startup or pursuing a career at an established company, Python opens up a range of opportunities.

Career Opportunities for Python Developers

Learning Python offers significant career opportunities across various fields, and its versatility ensures you'll never run out of interesting roles to pursue.

1. Web Development

Python plays a crucial role in web development. Popular frameworks like Django and Flask allow developers to quickly build dynamic, secure, and scalable websites and applications. Python's simplicity and scalability make it ideal for both small-scale projects and large-scale enterprise applications.

As a web developer, you'll be involved in the full development cycle, from setting up a web server to managing databases, handling user requests, and implementing security features. Python makes all of this much easier compared to other languages, allowing you to focus on building out the core functionality of the application.

2. Data Science and Machine Learning

Data science is one of the most sought-after fields in tech, and Python is the language of choice for data scientists and analysts. With powerful libraries like NumPy, pandas, and Matplotlib, Python makes data manipulation, analysis, and visualization straightforward.

Additionally, Python is at the core of machine learning. Libraries like scikit-learn and TensorFlow enable the development of machine learning models and neural networks, which are widely used for predictive analytics, automation, and even deep learning. With

Python, you can analyze data and build AI systems that have real-world applications, such as recommendation engines, fraud detection systems, and natural language processing models.

3. Automation and Scripting

Python is also widely used for automation tasks, saving time and effort in repetitive work. Whether it's automating daily workflows, managing data processing, or creating bots, Python's clean syntax and powerful libraries allow you to automate virtually anything. Automation specialists use Python to write scripts for tasks such as web scraping, file management, and system maintenance.

4. DevOps and Cloud Computing

DevOps is an increasingly important field in the tech industry, focusing on automating and streamlining the development and operations process. Python is a top language in DevOps due to its ease of use and flexibility. Python can be used to create automation scripts that manage deployment, monitor systems, and scale applications in cloud environments such as AWS or Google Cloud.

5. Game Development

Python is not the first language that comes to mind when thinking about game development, but it's certainly capable of creating simple 2D games and prototypes. The Pygame library allows developers to design games with graphics, sound, and interactivity. While not ideal for high-performance 3D gaming engines, Python is a great choice for hobbyists and beginners interested in game development.

Setting Up Your Development Environment

Before diving into Python programming, you need to set up the right tools. A proper development environment ensures that you have everything you need to write, test, and run your code. Let's take a look at how to get your system ready for Python development.

Installing Python

1. **Visit the Official Python Website**
   Go to python.org and download the latest version of Python for your operating system (Windows, macOS, or Linux). Python comes with a built-in package manager called `pip`, which helps you install additional libraries as needed.
2. **Install Python on Your System**
   Follow the installation steps provided on the website. Be sure to check the box to add Python to your system's PATH (this allows you to run Python from the command line). The installation process should only take a few minutes.
3. **Verify the Installation**
   After installation, open a terminal or command prompt and type `python --version` to ensure that Python has been installed correctly. You should see the Python version number displayed. If you see an error, revisit the installation process.

Setting Up a Code Editor (VS Code, PyCharm)

1. Visual Studio Code (VS Code)
VS Code is one of the most popular code editors for Python development. It's lightweight, fast, and has plenty of extensions to make coding easier.

- Install VS Code from visualstudio.com.
- Once installed, launch VS Code and open the extensions tab to search for and install the "Python" extension.

- This extension provides features like code completion, error detection, and debugging, making it ideal for Python development.

2. PyCharm

PyCharm is another excellent choice for Python development, especially for larger projects. It's an integrated development environment (IDE) that offers features such as project navigation, code refactoring, debugging, and more.

- Download PyCharm from jetbrains.com.
- The community edition is free, and it's sufficient for most Python development tasks.

Creating Your First Python Script

Now that your development environment is ready, it's time to write your first Python script. This simple "Hello, World!" program will introduce you to the basic structure of a Python program.

```python
print("Hello, World!")
```

When you run this script, Python will print "Hello, World!" to the console. This is your first step toward learning Python!

Explanation:

- `print()` is a built-in function in Python that outputs data to the screen.
- The string "Hello, World!" is enclosed in quotes because it's a string literal.

How to Use This Book: A Roadmap for Success

This book is designed to take you from beginner to Python pro, providing you with all the tools you need to succeed in the tech industry. Each chapter builds on the previous one, and by the end, you'll have a strong foundation in Python and be able to apply it to real-world projects.

Here's how you can maximize the value of this book:

- **Work on the Projects**: Every chapter includes practical projects to help you reinforce your learning. Don't skip them; they're the key to solidifying your skills.
- **Practice Consistently**: Python is best learned through practice. Try to write code every day, even if it's just a small script.
- **Ask for Help**: Join online forums, read Python blogs, and reach out to the Python community if you get stuck. You're not alone in this learning journey.
- **Build a Portfolio**: As you progress, start collecting your projects in a portfolio. This will be useful when applying for jobs in Python development.

Chapter 2: Your First Python Program

Understanding the Basics: Syntax and Structure

When it comes to programming, the first thing you'll need to understand is the language's syntax and structure. Think of syntax as the set of rules that govern how the code is written, just like grammar rules in English. Python is known for its readability, which makes it one of the best languages for beginners. Let's break down the structure that makes Python both beginner-friendly and powerful.

What is Syntax?

In any programming language, syntax refers to the way in which commands and statements are written. Each programming language has its own set of rules for how the code should be written, and understanding these rules is crucial to writing error-free programs. When you write code in Python, the language will check your syntax to ensure it's valid. If there are mistakes, Python will raise an error.

Python's syntax rules are designed to be simple and intuitive. This is one reason Python is widely recommended for people just starting out with programming. The key aspects of Python's syntax include:

1. **Indentation**: Python uses indentation (spaces or tabs) to define blocks of code, rather than curly braces { } as in languages like C, C++, or Java. For example, when defining functions or control flow (like loops and conditionals), Python relies on indentation to determine the structure. Each level of indentation usually consists of four spaces.

   Example:

```python

def greet():
    print("Hello, World!")
```

2. **Case Sensitivity**: Python is case-sensitive, meaning that `Variable`, `variable`, and `VARIABLE` are considered different identifiers.
3. **Comments**: Python allows you to include comments in your code, which are used to explain what the code is doing. Comments are ignored by Python and don't affect the program's behavior. They're important for making your code more readable.

Single-line comment:

```python

# This is a comment
```

Multi-line comment:

```python

'''
This is a multi-line comment
spanning across several lines.
'''
```

The Structure of a Python Program

At the most basic level, a Python program is made up of statements. A statement is an instruction that tells the computer to do something. These could be expressions, variable assignments, function calls, or condition checks.

Here's what a simple Python program looks like:

```python
# This is a simple Python program
name = "Alice"   # Variable assignment
print("Hello, " + name)   # Function call
```

This program has a variable assignment (name = "Alice") and a function call (print("Hello, " + name)) — both of which are essential parts of any Python program.

Working with Variables and Data Types

Variables are the building blocks of your program. A variable is a place to store data, which you can later reference or change. In Python, you don't need to specify the data type when you declare a variable. Python automatically determines the type of the variable based on the value assigned to it.

What Are Variables?

A variable is essentially a name given to a data value. Variables are used to store data that you can later manipulate or refer to. You can think of a variable as a labeled container in which you can store information. When you assign a value to a variable, Python stores that value in memory and associates it with the name you've chosen.

For example:

```python
x = 10   # x is now storing the value 10
name = "John"   # name is now storing the string
"John"
```

Data Types in Python

Python supports various data types, each suited for different kinds of data. Let's explore some of the most commonly used data types:

1. **Integers**: Whole numbers, positive or negative.

   ```python
   x = 10
   ```

2. **Floating-point numbers (floats)**: Numbers with decimal points.

   ```python
   pi = 3.14159
   ```

3. **Strings**: A sequence of characters, enclosed in either single or double quotes.

   ```python
   name = "Alice"
   greeting = 'Hello, Alice!'
   ```

4. **Booleans**: A data type that can only be either `True` or `False`.

   ```python
   is_active = True
   is_sunny = False
   ```

5. **Lists**: An ordered collection of items, which can be of any data type.

   ```python
   numbers = [1, 2, 3, 4]
   ```

6. **Tuples**: Similar to lists but immutable (unchangeable once created).

```python
colors = ("red", "green", "blue")
```

7. **Dictionaries**: Unordered collections of key-value pairs.

```python
person = {"name": "John", "age": 30}
```

Python also supports more complex data types and structures, but understanding these basic types is essential to get started. Let's now look at how to use these types in practical situations.

First Python Program: Hello, World!

Your first Python program is one of the simplest yet most significant milestones in your journey as a programmer: printing "Hello, World!" to the screen. This simple task is often the first step for beginners, as it demonstrates how to output data and interact with the user.

Why "Hello, World!"?

Printing "Hello, World!" serves as an introductory exercise to familiarize yourself with the syntax and structure of the Python language. It's a simple program that helps you understand the relationship between the code you write and the output you see.

Here's how to write it:

```python
# This is your first Python program
```

```python
print("Hello, World!")
```

Breakdown of the Code:

- `print()` is a built-in function in Python that outputs text to the screen.
- `"Hello, World!"` is a string that is being passed to the `print()` function.

When you run this program, Python will output `Hello, World!` to the console. It's a simple task, but it's a starting point for understanding how your program interacts with the world outside the code.

Common Errors and Troubleshooting

No matter how simple a program is, it's inevitable that you'll run into errors at some point. Errors are a part of the learning process, and understanding how to identify and troubleshoot them is a key skill in programming.

Common Errors in Python

1. **Syntax Errors**: These occur when Python detects a problem with the structure of the code. For example:

   ```python
   print("Hello, World!"  # Missing closing parenthesis
   ```

2. **Indentation Errors**: Python relies on indentation to define code blocks, so incorrect indentation can result in errors.

   ```python
   def greet():
   ```

```
print("Hello")   # Missing indentation
```

3. **Name Errors**: These happen when you try to use a variable or function that hasn't been defined yet.

```
python
```

```
print(name)   # NameError: name 'name' is not
defined
```

4. **Type Errors**: These occur when you try to perform an operation on incompatible data types.

```
python
```

```
x = "Hello"
y = 10
print(x + y)   # TypeError: can only concatenate
str (not "int") to str
```

Troubleshooting Tips

1. **Read the Error Message**: Python provides error messages that give you a clue about what went wrong. Understanding these messages is crucial for fixing bugs in your code.
2. **Use Print Statements**: If your program isn't behaving as expected, use `print()` statements to display the values of variables and help you understand what's happening at different stages of the code.
3. **Check for Typos**: Often, errors are simply due to small mistakes like misspelling a variable name or forgetting a punctuation mark.
4. **Use an IDE**: Tools like Visual Studio Code or PyCharm highlight syntax errors, which can save you time during troubleshooting.

Real-World Analogy: What Happens Behind the Code?

To understand how Python works behind the scenes, let's think of it as giving instructions to a robot. You tell the robot what to do in a language it understands, and it carries out the tasks you've assigned.

When you write a Python program, you're essentially giving a series of instructions to your computer. The computer doesn't "think" like we do; it just follows the rules of the language step by step.

Behind the Scenes:

1. **Writing the Code**: You type out instructions (the Python code) that tell the computer what to do. For instance, `print("Hello, World!")` tells the computer to output a message.
2. **Running the Code**: When you run the program, the Python interpreter translates the code into machine code (which the computer understands) and then executes it.
3. **Output**: Once the program runs, the result is displayed to you (in our case, the message "Hello, World!" on the screen). This is like giving the robot an instruction, and it responds by performing the task you asked.

Conclusion

This chapter covered the essentials of writing your first Python program, understanding the syntax and structure, and troubleshooting common errors. By now, you've learned how to create a basic Python script, manipulate data types, and identify and resolve errors. In the following chapters, we'll build upon these concepts and dive deeper into more advanced topics, but remember that every great programmer starts with these foundational steps.

Chapter 3: Control Flow and Decision Making

Introduction to Control Flow

Control flow refers to the order in which individual statements, instructions, or function calls are executed in a program. In any programming language, the flow of execution can be altered based on certain conditions or repetitive tasks. Python, like most programming languages, provides several tools to manage control flow: **conditional statements** and **loops**.

- **Conditional Statements**: These are the building blocks of decision-making in Python. They let you control the flow of execution depending on whether a certain condition is met.
- **Loops**: Loops allow you to repeat certain sections of your program for a specific number of times or while a condition is true.

In this chapter, we'll explore these fundamental concepts in detail, beginning with how to make decisions in your code and how to repeat tasks. We will also apply these concepts in a hands-on project that will involve creating a simple calculator.

If, Else, and Elif Statements

In Python, the **if** statement allows you to execute certain code based on a condition. If the condition evaluates to `True`, the block of code within the `if` statement will be executed. If not, the program will skip that block and move on to the next section of code.

The If Statement

The basic syntax of an `if` statement looks like this:

```python
if condition:
    # execute this block if condition is True
```

For example:

```python
age = 18
if age >= 18:
    print("You are an adult.")
```

Here, the program checks whether `age` is greater than or equal to 18. Since it is, the program prints "You are an adult."

The Else Statement

The `else` statement can be used in conjunction with an `if` statement to provide an alternative block of code when the condition is not met.

```python
if age >= 18:
    print("You are an adult.")
else:
    print("You are not an adult.")
```

In this case, if the `age` is less than 18, the program will print "You are not an adult."

The Elif Statement

The `elif` (short for "else if") statement is used when you want to check multiple conditions. If the first condition is not true, Python will check the next one.

python

```
age = 65
if age < 18:
    print("You are a minor.")
elif age < 65:
    print("You are an adult.")
else:
    print("You are a senior citizen.")
```

In this example, the `elif` checks if the `age` is less than 65, and if neither condition is true, the `else` statement is executed.

Loops: For Loops and While Loops

Loops are one of the most important tools in programming. They allow you to repeat certain blocks of code multiple times, which is essential for reducing redundancy and increasing efficiency.

For Loops

A `for` loop is used to iterate over a sequence, such as a list, tuple, dictionary, string, or range. This loop repeats the block of code for each item in the sequence.

Example of a For Loop:
python

```
for i in range(5):  # range(5) creates a sequence of
numbers from 0 to 4
    print(i)
```

Output:

```
0
1
2
3
4
```

In this example, the `for` loop iterates over the numbers from 0 to 4 and prints each one. The `range()` function generates a sequence of numbers, and the loop executes the print statement for each number in the range.

For Loop with a List:
python

```
names = ["Alice", "Bob", "Charlie"]
for name in names:
    print(name)
```

This will output:

```
nginx
```

```
Alice
Bob
Charlie
```

While Loops

A `while` loop repeatedly executes a block of code as long as the specified condition is true. It's different from a `for` loop in that you define the condition explicitly, and the loop will continue until that condition is no longer true.

Example of a While Loop:
python

```
i = 0
```

```
while i < 5:
    print(i)
    i += 1   # increment i by 1
```

Output:

```
0
1
2
3
4
```

In this example, the `while` loop continues to run as long as `i` is less than 5. The loop will print the value of `i` and then increment it by 1 after each iteration. If `i` becomes 5, the condition `i < 5` will be false, and the loop will stop.

Infinite Loops

If you forget to update the variable that controls the condition in a `while` loop, it can lead to an **infinite loop**. Here's an example:

```python
i = 0
while i < 5:
    print(i)
```

This will print `0` indefinitely because `i` is never incremented. Be careful when using `while` loops to ensure that the condition will eventually evaluate to `False`.

Handling User Input

One of the most common ways to interact with users in a program is through user input. Python provides the `input()` function to handle this.

Using the `input()` Function

The `input()` function waits for the user to type something into the console. Once the user hits `Enter`, the function returns the input as a string.

```python
name = input("Enter your name: ")
print("Hello, " + name)
```

Output:

```yaml
Enter your name: Alice
Hello, Alice
```

In this example, Python prompts the user to enter their name, stores the input in the variable `name`, and then prints a personalized greeting.

Converting User Input

Since the `input()` function always returns data as a string, you often need to convert the input to the appropriate data type.

For example, if you ask the user for a number, you'll need to convert the input to an integer:

```python
```

```python
age = int(input("Enter your age: "))
print("You are " + str(age) + " years old.")
```

The `int()` function converts the string input into an integer so that you can perform mathematical operations on it.

Project: Build a Simple Calculator

Let's put everything you've learned so far into practice by building a simple calculator. This calculator will take user input and perform basic arithmetic operations like addition, subtraction, multiplication, and division.

Step 1: Define Functions for Operations

We will create separate functions for each arithmetic operation to keep the code organized.

python

```python
def add(x, y):
    return x + y

def subtract(x, y):
    return x - y

def multiply(x, y):
    return x * y

def divide(x, y):
    if y == 0:
        return "Error! Division by zero."
    return x / y
```

Step 2: Handle User Input for Operations

We will prompt the user to select an operation and then ask for two numbers. Based on the user's choice, we will call the appropriate function.

python

```python
def calculator():
    print("Select operation:")
    print("1. Add")
    print("2. Subtract")
    print("3. Multiply")
    print("4. Divide")

    choice = input("Enter choice (1/2/3/4): ")

    num1 = float(input("Enter first number: "))
    num2 = float(input("Enter second number: "))

    if choice == '1':
        print(num1, "+", num2, "=", add(num1, num2))
    elif choice == '2':
        print(num1, "-", num2, "=", subtract(num1,
num2))
    elif choice == '3':
        print(num1, "*", num2, "=", multiply(num1,
num2))
    elif choice == '4':
        print(num1, "/", num2, "=", divide(num1,
num2))
    else:
        print("Invalid Input")
```

Step 3: Run the Calculator

Finally, we'll call the `calculator()` function to start the program.

python

```python
calculator()
```

Now, when you run the program, it will prompt the user for input and perform the desired arithmetic operation.

Decision-Making Structures for Operations (Addition, Subtraction, etc.)

In the calculator program above, the decision-making structure was implemented using **if-else statements**. Based on the user's input (whether they choose addition, subtraction, multiplication, or division), the program decides which function to call and performs the corresponding operation.

In more complex programs, you may have several conditions that need to be checked before taking action. For example, if you're working with multiple operations or conditions that could conflict, using decision structures helps your program know which action to prioritize.

Debugging Techniques: Common Pitfalls

Even experienced programmers make mistakes. Debugging is an essential skill for every developer. Let's go over some common pitfalls and how to avoid them.

1. Incorrect Input Handling

A common mistake is not properly handling user input. If you ask the user for a number but don't convert the input to the appropriate type (like `int()` or `float()`), you'll get errors.

Solution: Always ensure that input is properly validated and converted before using it.

2. Infinite Loops

Forgetting to update the condition in a `while` loop is a classic mistake. This can lead to the program running forever, consuming resources and making it unresponsive.

Solution: Ensure that the condition will eventually be met to terminate the loop.

3. Off-by-One Errors in Loops

When working with loops, sometimes you might accidentally skip over or repeat one iteration. This is called an off-by-one error and typically occurs when dealing with ranges or list indices.

Solution: Double-check your loop boundaries and ensure that your conditions are accurate.

4. Indentation Errors

Python relies on indentation to define blocks of code. Mixing tabs and spaces or inconsistent indentation can lead to errors that are often hard to spot.

Solution: Stick to four spaces for indentation and avoid mixing tabs and spaces.

Conclusion

In this chapter, we've covered the essentials of control flow, including `if`, `else`, and `elif` statements, as well as loops (`for` and `while`). We also built a simple calculator that incorporated user input and decision-making structures for performing arithmetic operations. These tools are the foundation of any programming language, and mastering them will allow you to create more complex and interactive programs.

Chapter 4: Data Structures: Lists, Tuples, and Dictionaries

Introduction to Data Structures in Python

In Python, data structures are ways to organize and store data so that it can be accessed and manipulated efficiently. Understanding how to use these structures effectively is crucial to becoming a proficient Python developer. There are several data structures in Python, but in this chapter, we'll focus on three of the most commonly used ones:

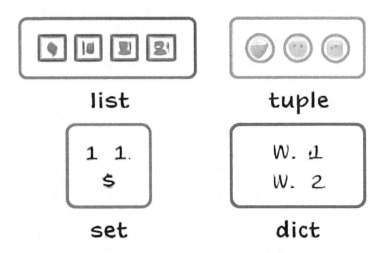

- **Lists:** Ordered collections of items, which can be changed or manipulated.
- **Tuples:** Similar to lists but immutable; once created, they cannot be altered.

- **Dictionaries**: Unordered collections of key-value pairs that allow for fast lookups.

Each of these data structures has specific use cases, and understanding when and how to use them is a core skill for any Python developer.

Understanding Lists and Indexing

A **list** in Python is an ordered collection of items. Lists are one of the most versatile data structures in Python because they allow you to store elements of different data types (such as integers, strings, and even other lists) in a single variable.

Creating a List

You can create a list by placing items inside square brackets [ ], separated by commas.

python

```python
fruits = ["apple", "banana", "cherry"]
print(fruits)
```

This list contains three strings: `"apple"`, `"banana"`, and `"cherry"`. Lists can store items of different data types:

python

```python
mixed_list = [1, "hello", 3.14, True]
print(mixed_list)
```

Indexing Lists

Each item in a list is associated with an index. The index starts at 0 for the first item, 1 for the second item, and so on. You can access any item in the list by using its index.

```python
python
```

```python
fruits = ["apple", "banana", "cherry"]
print(fruits[0])   # Outputs: apple
```

Negative indices are also allowed in Python. A negative index starts counting from the end of the list. For example, -1 refers to the last item in the list.

```python
python
```

```python
print(fruits[-1])   # Outputs: cherry
```

Modifying Lists

Since lists are mutable (i.e., they can be changed), you can modify the items in a list by directly accessing the index.

```python
python
```

```python
fruits[1] = "blueberry"
print(fruits)   # Outputs: ['apple', 'blueberry', 'cherry']
```

You can also add new items to the list using the append() method or insert an item at a specific position with insert().

```python
python
```

```python
fruits.append("orange")   # Adds "orange" to the end of the list
fruits.insert(1, "kiwi")   # Inserts "kiwi" at the second position
print(fruits)   # Outputs: ['apple', 'kiwi', 'blueberry', 'cherry', 'orange']
```

Removing Items from a List

Python provides several methods to remove items from a list. For instance, remove() deletes the first occurrence of a specified item, while pop() removes an item at a given index (and returns it).

```python
```

```python
fruits.remove("kiwi")  # Removes the first occurrence
of "kiwi"
popped_fruit = fruits.pop(1)  # Removes and returns
the item at index 1
print(fruits)  # Outputs: ['apple', 'blueberry',
'cherry', 'orange']
print(popped_fruit)  # Outputs: blueberry
```

You can also clear the entire list using the `clear()` method:

```python
```

```python
fruits.clear()  # Clears all items from the list
print(fruits)  # Outputs: []
```

Manipulating Tuples: When to Use Them

A **tuple** is similar to a list in Python but is **immutable**. Once a tuple is created, its elements cannot be changed, added, or removed. Tuples are used when you want to ensure that the data remains constant throughout the program.

Creating a Tuple

Tuples are defined by using parentheses `()` instead of square brackets `[]`. The elements of a tuple are separated by commas.

```python
```

```python
coordinates = (10.0, 20.0)
print(coordinates)
```

In this example, `coordinates` is a tuple containing two float values. Just like lists, tuples can hold data of different types.

```python
```

```
mixed_tuple = (1, "hello", 3.14, False)
print(mixed_tuple)
```

Accessing Tuple Elements

Since tuples are ordered, you can access elements using an index, just like with lists:

python

```
print(coordinates[0])   # Outputs: 10.0
print(coordinates[1])   # Outputs: 20.0
```

Negative indexing also works with tuples:

python

```
print(coordinates[-1])   # Outputs: 20.0
```

Why Use Tuples?

Since tuples are immutable, they are faster than lists when it comes to iteration. Tuples also make a good choice when you need a data structure that should not be modified after creation. For example, tuples are often used to represent fixed collections of data, like coordinates, RGB color values, or other fixed-size groups of items.

Tuples are also hashable, which means they can be used as keys in dictionaries (whereas lists cannot).

Dictionaries: Key-Value Pairs

A **dictionary** in Python is an unordered collection of **key-value pairs**. Unlike lists and tuples, dictionaries are indexed by **keys**, which can be any immutable data type (such as strings, integers, or tuples). Values associated with keys can be of any data type.

Creating a Dictionary

You create a dictionary by enclosing key-value pairs in curly braces {}, with a colon separating the key and the value.

```python
contact = {"name": "Alice", "phone": "123-456-7890",
"email": "alice@example.com"}
print(contact)
```

Accessing Values in a Dictionary

You can access the value associated with a key by using square brackets and the key name.

```python
print(contact["name"])   # Outputs: Alice
```

If you try to access a key that doesn't exist in the dictionary, Python will raise a KeyError. To avoid this, you can use the get() method, which returns None if the key doesn't exist.

```python
print(contact.get("address", "Not available"))   #
Outputs: Not available
```

Modifying and Adding Items

You can modify the value associated with an existing key by reassigning it:

```python
contact["phone"] = "987-654-3210"
print(contact["phone"])   # Outputs: 987-654-3210
```

You can also add new key-value pairs to a dictionary:

```python
```

```python
contact["address"] = "123 Main St."
print(contact)
```

Removing Items

To remove a key-value pair from a dictionary, you can use the `del` statement or the `pop()` method. The `pop()` method also returns the value associated with the key.

```python
```

```python
del contact["email"]
print(contact)

email = contact.pop("phone")
print(email)   # Outputs: 987-654-3210
```

Iterating Over a Dictionary

You can iterate over the keys, values, or key-value pairs of a dictionary using a `for` loop.

```python
```

```python
# Iterating over keys
for key in contact:
    print(key)

# Iterating over values
for value in contact.values():
    print(value)

# Iterating over key-value pairs
for key, value in contact.items():
    print(key, value)
```

Project: Create a Contact Book Using a Dictionary

In this project, you will create a simple contact book application using a Python dictionary. The dictionary will store contact information where the **name** is the key and the **phone number** is the value.

Step 1: Define the Contact Book

Start by creating an empty dictionary to store your contacts.

python

```python
contacts = {}
```

Step 2: Add Contacts

Create a function to add a new contact to the dictionary.

python

```python
def add_contact(name, phone_number):
    contacts[name] = phone_number
```

Now, you can add contacts to your contact book.

python

```python
add_contact("Alice", "123-456-7890")
add_contact("Bob", "987-654-3210")
```

Step 3: Display Contacts

Create a function to display all contacts in the contact book.

python

```python
def display_contacts():
```

```python
    for name, phone in contacts.items():
        print(f"{name}: {phone}")
```

Step 4: Search for a Contact

Create a function to search for a contact by name.

python

```python
def search_contact(name):
    if name in contacts:
        print(f"{name}: {contacts[name]}")
    else:
        print(f"Contact {name} not found.")
```

Step 5: Delete a Contact

Create a function to delete a contact from the contact book.

python

```python
def delete_contact(name):
    if name in contacts:
        del contacts[name]
        print(f"Contact {name} deleted.")
    else:
        print(f"Contact {name} not found.")
```

Step 6: Test the Contact Book

Now, you can test your contact book by adding, displaying, searching, and deleting contacts.

python

```python
add_contact("Alice", "123-456-7890")
add_contact("Bob", "987-654-3210")
display_contacts()
search_contact("Alice")
delete_contact("Bob")
display_contacts()
```

Best Practices for Data Storage in Python

While Python provides powerful data structures like lists, tuples, and dictionaries, choosing the right one for your application is essential for efficient performance and maintainability. Here are some best practices:

1. Choose the Right Data Structure for the Task

- Use **lists** when you need an ordered collection of items and may need to modify it (add/remove elements).
- Use **tuples** when you have a fixed collection of items that should not change.
- Use **dictionaries** when you need fast lookups by key or need to associate values with keys.

2. Avoid Using Lists for Key-Value Pairs

- If you need to store data as key-value pairs, **dictionaries** are much more efficient than using lists, especially when the dataset grows larger.

3. Use List Comprehensions

- Python supports a compact and efficient way to create lists using **list comprehensions**. They allow you to build lists in a single line of code.

```python
squares = [x**2 for x in range(10)]
```

4. Keep Data Structures Simple

- Try to use simple, straightforward data structures where possible. Avoid nesting too many complex structures, as it can make your code harder to read and maintain.

5. Leverage Built-In Functions

- Python offers many built-in methods for data manipulation. Take advantage of methods like `sort()`, `reverse()`, `clear()`, and others to manipulate lists and dictionaries efficiently.

Conclusion

In this chapter, we've explored the fundamentals of Python's most commonly used data structures: **lists, tuples**, and **dictionaries**. Each of these data structures has its unique use case, and understanding when to use each one will help you write efficient and maintainable code. You've also learned how to create a contact book using a dictionary, which demonstrates the power of key-value pair storage in real-world applications.

By mastering these core data structures, you'll be well-equipped to handle more complex programming challenges in Python.

Chapter 5: Functions and Modular Programming

Introduction to Functions and Modular Programming

In programming, **functions** are one of the core concepts that allow you to break down complex tasks into manageable pieces. Functions enable you to group together blocks of code that perform a specific task and can be reused throughout your program. This concept is key to writing clean, efficient, and reusable code.

Modular programming is a design principle that emphasizes breaking down a program into smaller, self-contained modules. These modules can be functions, classes, or libraries. By focusing on small units of work, modular programming makes your code more maintainable and scalable.

In this chapter, we'll dive deep into the concept of functions in Python. We'll look at why functions matter, how to define and call them, and how to work with arguments and return values. Then, we'll apply what we've learned in a hands-on project where we build a simple to-do list application using functions.

Why Functions Matter: Reusability and Efficiency

One of the most important reasons to use functions in your programs is that they help make your code more **reusable** and **efficient**. Functions allow you to define a piece of logic once and then reuse it whenever you need it, instead of duplicating code throughout your program.

1. Reusability

Reusability is a key benefit of functions. Once a function is written and tested, it can be used throughout your program without having to rewrite the same code multiple times.

For example, if you need to calculate the area of a circle in multiple places in your program, instead of writing the formula every time, you can define a function to handle this calculation:

python

```python
def area_of_circle(radius):
    return 3.14 * radius ** 2
```

You can then call the function whenever you need to calculate the area:

python

```python
print(area_of_circle(5))    # Outputs: 78.5
```

This makes your code cleaner, easier to read, and more efficient.

2. Efficiency

Functions help to reduce **redundancy**. Without functions, you would need to repeat the same blocks of code for every task that needs to be done. This increases the likelihood of errors and makes it harder to maintain and modify your code.

By defining a function once, you only have to update it in one place if changes are needed, rather than tracking down every instance of that block of code.

Functions also help you **organize** your code. Instead of having one large block of code doing everything, functions divide your program into smaller, logically separated pieces. This makes it easier to debug and maintain your code.

Defining and Calling Functions

1. Defining a Function

In Python, a function is defined using the `def` keyword followed by the function name and parentheses `()`. The parentheses may contain parameters (also called arguments) that the function can accept. The body of the function is indented and contains the statements that will be executed when the function is called.

Here's an example of a simple function definition:

python

```python
def greet():
    print("Hello, World!")
```

In this case, the function `greet()` doesn't take any parameters. It simply prints `"Hello, World!"` when called.

2. Calling a Function

Once a function is defined, you can call it by using its name followed by parentheses:

python

```python
greet()   # Outputs: Hello, World!
```

You can call a function as many times as needed throughout your program.

3. Function with Arguments

Sometimes, a function needs to accept data to work with. You can pass values into a function using **parameters** or **arguments**. These values allow the function to work with dynamic data.

Here's an example of a function that accepts an argument:

python

```python
def greet(name):
    print(f"Hello, {name}!")
```

In this case, the function takes one parameter (`name`). When you call the function, you pass a value for `name`:

python

```python
greet("Alice")   # Outputs: Hello, Alice!
greet("Bob")   # Outputs: Hello, Bob!
```

4. Function with Multiple Arguments

A function can accept multiple arguments, separated by commas:

python

```python
def greet(name, age):
    print(f"Hello, {name}! You are {age} years old.")
```

Now, when you call the function, you need to provide two values:

python

```python
greet("Alice", 30)   # Outputs: Hello, Alice! You are
30 years old.
```

5. Returning a Value from a Function

A function can return a value using the `return` keyword. The `return` statement allows a function to send data back to the place where it was called.

Here's an example of a function that returns a value:

```python
def add(x, y):
    return x + y
```

Now, you can call the function and store the result in a variable:

```python
result = add(5, 3)
print(result)   # Outputs: 8
```

Functions that return values are useful when you need to perform calculations or retrieve information that will be used elsewhere in the program.

Arguments and Return Values

1. Positional Arguments

In Python, the most common way to pass data into a function is by using **positional arguments**. These are arguments that are assigned values based on their position when the function is called. The first argument is assigned to the first parameter, the second argument to the second parameter, and so on.

For example:

```python
python

def subtract(x, y):
    return x - y

result = subtract(10, 5)   # 10 is assigned to x, 5 is
assigned to y
print(result)   # Outputs: 5
```

2. Keyword Arguments

Keyword arguments allow you to pass data into a function by specifying the name of the parameter. This is helpful when calling functions with many parameters, as it allows you to explicitly define which argument corresponds to which parameter.

Here's an example:

```python
python

def greet(name, age):
    print(f"Hello, {name}! You are {age} years old.")

greet(age=30, name="Alice")   # Outputs: Hello, Alice!
You are 30 years old.
```

Using keyword arguments makes your function calls more readable and helps avoid errors when passing the wrong values to parameters.

3. Default Arguments

In some cases, you might want a parameter to have a default value if the caller doesn't provide one. You can do this by assigning a default value to the parameter when defining the function.

```python
python

def greet(name, age=25):
    print(f"Hello, {name}! You are {age} years old.")
```

```
greet("Alice")  # Outputs: Hello, Alice! You are 25
years old.
greet("Bob", 30)  # Outputs: Hello, Bob! You are 30
years old.
```

In this case, if age is not provided, it defaults to 25.

Project: Build a Simple To-Do List with Functions

In this project, we'll create a simple to-do list application using functions. This will allow us to practice defining and calling functions, passing arguments, and working with return values.

Step 1: Define the Functions

We'll need several functions to handle different actions in our to-do list:

- **add_task**: Adds a task to the list.
- **remove_task**: Removes a task from the list.
- **view_tasks**: Displays all tasks in the list.

```python
# Initialize an empty to-do list
todo_list = []

def add_task(task):
    todo_list.append(task)
    print(f"Task '{task}' added.")

def remove_task(task):
    if task in todo_list:
        todo_list.remove(task)
        print(f"Task '{task}' removed.")
    else:
```

```
        print(f"Task '{task}' not found.")

def view_tasks():
    if todo_list:
        print("To-Do List:")
        for task in todo_list:
            print(f"- {task}")
    else:
        print("Your to-do list is empty.")
```

Step 2: Create a Simple User Interface

Next, we'll create a simple loop that allows the user to interact with the to-do list. The user can add, remove, or view tasks by choosing an option from a menu.

```python
def main():
    while True:
        print("\nTo-Do List Menu:")
        print("1. Add Task")
        print("2. Remove Task")
        print("3. View Tasks")
        print("4. Exit")

        choice = input("Enter your choice: ")

        if choice == "1":
            task = input("Enter the task to add: ")
            add_task(task)
        elif choice == "2":
            task = input("Enter the task to remove:
")
            remove_task(task)
        elif choice == "3":
            view_tasks()
        elif choice == "4":
            print("Goodbye!")
            break
        else:
            print("Invalid choice. Please try
again.")
```

Step 3: Run the To-Do List Application

Now, you can run the application by calling the `main()` function.

python

```python
if __name__ == "__main__":
    main()
```

This simple to-do list application allows the user to add, remove, and view tasks. Functions help us to keep the code organized, making it easier to maintain and update.

Understanding Scope and Lifetime of Variables

1. Local Scope

In Python, variables defined inside a function are considered to have **local scope**. This means that the variable is only accessible within the function where it was created. Once the function finishes executing, the local variable is no longer available.

python

```python
def example_function():
    x = 10   # x is a local variable
    print(x)

example_function()   # Outputs: 10
print(x)   # Raises a NameError, because x is not
accessible outside the function
```

2. Global Scope

A variable defined outside of any function is considered to have **global scope**. This means the variable can be accessed by any function in the program.

```python
python

x = 10   # x is a global variable

def example_function():
    print(x)

example_function()   # Outputs: 10
```

3. Lifetime of Variables

The **lifetime** of a variable refers to how long the variable exists in memory. Local variables are created when the function is called and destroyed when the function exits. Global variables, on the other hand, exist for the duration of the program.

4. Modifying Global Variables Inside a Function

To modify a global variable inside a function, you need to declare it as global using the global keyword.

```python
python

x = 10

def modify_global():
    global x
    x = 20

modify_global()
print(x)   # Outputs: 20
```

Without the global keyword, Python will treat the variable as a local variable, which can lead to errors or unexpected behavior.

Conclusion

In this chapter, we've covered the essentials of **functions** in Python, including why they matter for reusability and efficiency. We've learned how to define and call functions, work with arguments and return values, and explore the concepts of **scope** and **lifetime** of variables. We also applied these concepts by building a simple to-do list application that uses functions to manage tasks.

By mastering functions, you can make your code more modular, readable, and reusable, which is a critical skill for both small and large-scale programming projects.

Chapter 6: Handling Errors and Exceptions

Introduction to Error Handling in Python

In any software application, errors are inevitable. When writing code, you may encounter unexpected situations, such as trying to open a file that doesn't exist or attempting to divide a number by zero. These errors can cause the program to crash or behave unpredictably, making it difficult to maintain and use.

In Python, the process of **handling errors** and **exceptions** is essential for writing robust and reliable code. Python offers a sophisticated error handling mechanism that helps developers identify and fix problems without stopping the execution of the program. This process is known as **exception handling**.

In this chapter, we will explore the following concepts:

1. **Types of Errors in Python**: Understanding the different errors that can occur in your code.
2. **Using Try and Except**: How to catch and handle exceptions gracefully.
3. **Raising Exceptions**: How to create custom exceptions to handle specific scenarios in your application.
4. **Project**: Building a Robust File Reader Application.
5. **Best Practices for Writing Stable Code**: Ensuring that your code can handle errors without breaking.

By the end of this chapter, you'll be equipped with the knowledge to anticipate and handle errors effectively, leading to more reliable and maintainable code.

Types of Errors in Python

Python recognizes several types of errors, each indicating a different kind of problem. It's essential to understand these errors so that you can write code that anticipates and handles them correctly.

1. Syntax Errors

A **syntax error** occurs when Python cannot parse your code because it doesn't follow the correct syntax rules. Syntax errors are usually easy to spot, as Python will point them out in the error message.

For example:

```python
print("Hello World"  # Missing closing parenthesis
```

This will raise a syntax error:

```javascript
SyntaxError: unexpected EOF while parsing
```

To fix this, you simply need to correct the syntax, like so:

```python
print("Hello World")  # Correct syntax
```

2. Runtime Errors

A **runtime error** occurs while the program is running. These errors are harder to predict because they depend on the input or state of the program during execution. Examples of runtime errors include division by zero or trying to access a non-existent file.

For example:

```python
result = 10 / 0  # Division by zero
```

This will raise a `ZeroDivisionError`:

```vbnet
ZeroDivisionError: division by zero
```

3. Logical Errors

A **logical error** occurs when the program runs without crashing, but the output is not what you expected. These errors are the hardest to spot because Python doesn't raise an exception—they are usually the result of faulty logic or incorrect assumptions.

For example, if you forget to multiply in an equation:

```python
# Incorrect logic
total = 10 + 5  # The correct logic should be
multiplication, not addition
```

Although this doesn't raise an error, it produces incorrect results. Logical errors can be difficult to debug, but thorough testing and code review can help identify and fix them.

Using Try and Except for Error Handling

Python provides a powerful and simple way to handle errors using `try` and `except` blocks. This allows you to catch and handle exceptions, preventing your program from crashing.

1. The Try Block

The `try` block contains code that may raise an exception. You write the code that might cause an error inside the `try` block. If no error occurs, the code runs as usual. If an error occurs, Python jumps to the `except` block.

```python
```

```
try:
    x = 10 / 0   # This will raise a ZeroDivisionError
except ZeroDivisionError:
    print("Error: Cannot divide by zero.")
```

In this example, we attempt to divide by zero, which would normally raise an error. But because we've wrapped the code in a `try` block, Python catches the error and prints a friendly message instead of crashing.

2. The Except Block

The `except` block is used to define how to handle a specific error. You can specify the type of error you want to catch, or catch all errors by using a general `except` block.

Here's an example of catching a specific error:

```python
python
```

```
try:
    num = int(input("Enter a number: "))
    print(10 / num)
except ZeroDivisionError:
    print("Error: Cannot divide by zero.")
except ValueError:
    print("Error: Invalid input. Please enter a
number.")
```

In this example:

- If the user enters 0, the program will print `"Error: Cannot divide by zero."`.
- If the user enters something that cannot be converted to an integer (like a letter), the program will print `"Error: Invalid input. Please enter a number."`.

3. Catching Multiple Exceptions

You can catch multiple exceptions by adding multiple `except` blocks:

python

```
try:
    num = int(input("Enter a number: "))
    result = 10 / num
except ZeroDivisionError:
    print("Error: Cannot divide by zero.")
except ValueError:
    print("Error: Invalid input.")
```

In this example, if the user enters an invalid value, the `ValueError` block will catch it, and if the user tries to divide by zero, the `ZeroDivisionError` block will catch it.

4. The Else Block

An `else` block can be used after the `try` and `except` blocks. Code inside the `else` block runs if no exception is raised.

python

```
try:
    num = int(input("Enter a number: "))
    result = 10 / num
except ZeroDivisionError:
    print("Error: Cannot divide by zero.")
except ValueError:
    print("Error: Invalid input.")
else:
    print("The result is", result)
```

Here, if no exception occurs, the program will display the result of the division.

5. The Finally Block

The `finally` block is always executed, regardless of whether an exception occurred or not. This is useful for cleaning up resources, such as closing files or releasing network connections.

python

```
try:
    file = open("example.txt", "r")
    content = file.read()
except FileNotFoundError:
    print("Error: File not found.")
finally:
    file.close()  # Ensure the file is closed
regardless of errors
```

Raising Exceptions: Custom Errors

Sometimes, you may want to raise your own exceptions based on certain conditions in your program. Python provides the `raise` statement, which allows you to trigger an exception manually.

1. Raising Built-in Exceptions

You can raise built-in exceptions using the `raise` statement. For example:

python

```
x = -1
if x < 0:
    raise ValueError("x cannot be negative")
```

This will raise a `ValueError` with a custom message.

2. Creating Custom Exceptions

You can also create your own exceptions by subclassing Python's built-in `Exception` class. This is useful when you want to define specific error conditions in your program.

python

```python
class NegativeNumberError(Exception):
    def __init__(self, message):
        self.message = message
        super().__init__(self.message)

def check_number(x):
    if x < 0:
        raise NegativeNumberError("Negative numbers
are not allowed")
    return x

try:
    check_number(-5)
except NegativeNumberError as e:
    print(f"Custom Error: {e}")
```

In this example, we created a custom exception `NegativeNumberError` to handle cases where a negative number is encountered.

Project: Building a Robust File Reader Application

Let's now apply what we've learned by building a simple file reader application that handles errors effectively.

1. The Requirements

We'll write a program that:

- Opens and reads a file.
- Handles common errors like the file not being found.
- Displays proper error messages.
- Provides a graceful exit without crashing the program.

2. Reading a File Safely

The first step is to try opening the file and reading its contents. If the file doesn't exist, we'll catch the `FileNotFoundError` and display a custom error message.

python

```python
def read_file(filename):
    try:
        with open(filename, 'r') as file:
            content = file.read()
            print(content)
    except FileNotFoundError:
        print(f"Error: The file '{filename}' does not
exist.")
    except Exception as e:
        print(f"An unexpected error occurred: {e}")
```

In this code:

- We use a `with` statement to open the file, which ensures that the file is automatically closed when we're done.
- If the file is not found, the program will print an error message instead of crashing.

3. Handling Other Errors

Sometimes, the file may exist but there could be other issues, such as incorrect file format or permissions. We catch any general exceptions and provide a message.

python

```python
def read_file(filename):
    try:
        with open(filename, 'r') as file:
            content = file.read()
            print(content)
    except FileNotFoundError:
        print(f"Error: The file '{filename}' does not
exist.")
    except PermissionError:
        print(f"Error: You do not have permission to
access '{filename}'.")
    except Exception as e:
        print(f"An unexpected error occurred: {e}")
```

4. Testing the Application

Now, let's test our file reader with different scenarios:

1. A file that doesn't exist.
2. A file with permission errors.
3. A valid file.

```python
python
```

```python
read_file("nonexistent_file.txt")
read_file("restricted_file.txt")
read_file("valid_file.txt")
```

By running these tests, we ensure that the program handles various errors without crashing and provides useful error messages.

Best Practices for Writing Stable Code

Writing stable, error-free code requires planning and attention to detail. Here are some best practices to help you handle errors effectively in Python:

1. Use Specific Exceptions

Whenever possible, catch specific exceptions rather than using a generic `except Exception`. This makes your error handling more precise and helps with debugging.

```python
try:
    # Some code
except ZeroDivisionError:
    print("Cannot divide by zero.")
except FileNotFoundError:
    print("File not found.")
```

2. Graceful Degradation

Your program should handle errors in such a way that it degrades gracefully. Instead of crashing, it should handle the error and continue running, or at least exit with a clear message explaining what went wrong.

3. Don't Overuse Exceptions

Exceptions are a powerful tool, but they should not be used for flow control in your program. Use exceptions for truly exceptional cases, not for normal control flow.

4. Log Errors

In production environments, logging errors is crucial for troubleshooting. Python's `logging` module allows you to log error messages to a file, which can be reviewed later.

```python
import logging
```

```
logging.basicConfig(filename='app.log',
level=logging.ERROR)

try:
    # Some code that may raise an error
except Exception as e:
    logging.error(f"Error: {e}")
```

5. Test Thoroughly

Finally, always test your code under various conditions, including edge cases. Testing will help you uncover errors that may not be immediately obvious.

Conclusion

In this chapter, we've covered the essential concepts of error handling in Python. We learned how to handle errors using `try` and `except`, how to raise custom exceptions, and how to build a file reader application that gracefully handles errors.

By mastering error handling and exceptions, you can ensure that your Python programs are robust, reliable, and user-friendly

Chapter 7: Working with Files: Reading and Writing Data

Introduction to File Handling in Python

Working with files is one of the most common tasks in programming. Files are used to store data persistently—allowing you to access, modify, and save data between different runs of your program. Python provides built-in functionality for reading from and writing to files, making it easy to manage file-based data.

This chapter will cover the following topics:

1. **Reading Files**: How to open and read data from `.txt`, `.csv`, and `.json` files.
2. **Writing Data to Files**: How to save data to files, ensuring it's written in the right format.
3. **File Operations**: How to open, close, and update files.
4. **Project**: Building a CSV Expense Tracker.
5. **Understanding File Paths and Handling Directories**: How to work with file paths, directories, and relative paths.

By the end of this chapter, you will have a strong understanding of how to read and write files in Python, allowing you to work with data that's stored outside your program.

Reading Files: .txt, .csv, and .json

Reading files is the first step in working with file-based data. Python provides simple tools for opening and reading files of different formats. Let's explore how to handle different types of files commonly used in data processing.

1. Reading Text Files (.txt)

The simplest type of file to work with is a text file, commonly ending with `.txt`. You can use Python's built-in `open()` function to read text files. The `open()` function returns a file object, which you can then use to read the content of the file.

Opening a Text File for Reading

Here's an example of how to open a `.txt` file and read its content:

python

```
# Open the file for reading
file = open("sample.txt", "r")

# Read the content of the file
content = file.read()

# Print the content
print(content)

# Close the file after reading
file.close()
```

In this example:

- `"r"` stands for **read mode**, which means the file will only be opened for reading.
- `file.read()` reads the entire content of the file.
- After reading the file, it's important to **close** the file with `file.close()` to free up system resources.

Reading Line by Line

If the file is large, it's better to read it line by line to avoid loading the entire content into memory. You can use `file.readline()` or loop through the file object.

```python
file = open("sample.txt", "r")

# Read the file line by line
for line in file:
    print(line.strip())  # strip() removes
leading/trailing whitespaces

file.close()
```

2. Reading CSV Files (.csv)

CSV (Comma Separated Values) files are a common format for storing tabular data. Python's `csv` module makes it easy to read and write CSV files.

Reading a CSV File

To read a CSV file, you can use the `csv.reader` function from the `csv` module. Here's an example:

```python
import csv

# Open the CSV file for reading
with open("data.csv", mode="r") as file:
    csv_reader = csv.reader(file)

    # Read the header (optional)
    header = next(csv_reader)

    # Read each row in the CSV file
    for row in csv_reader:
```

```
    print(row)
```

In this example:

- `csv.reader()` returns a reader object that you can loop over to access each row in the CSV file.
- The `next()` function is used to skip the header row if it exists.

Handling CSV with Custom Delimiters

CSV files may use different delimiters (e.g., semicolons instead of commas). You can specify the delimiter by passing it as a parameter to `csv.reader()`.

python

```python
with open("data.csv", mode="r") as file:
    csv_reader = csv.reader(file, delimiter=";")
    for row in csv_reader:
        print(row)
```

3. Reading JSON Files (.json)

JSON (JavaScript Object Notation) is a popular format for storing and exchanging data, especially in web applications. Python's `json` module provides an easy way to work with JSON data.

Reading a JSON File

Here's how to read a JSON file and parse it into Python objects (like dictionaries or lists):

python

```python
import json

# Open the JSON file for reading
with open("data.json", "r") as file:
```

```
    data = json.load(file)

# Print the parsed JSON data
print(data)
```

In this example:

- `json.load(file)` parses the JSON data from the file and converts it into Python data structures (typically dictionaries or lists).
- The `with` statement ensures the file is properly closed after reading.

Writing Data to Files

Writing to files in Python involves opening a file in the appropriate mode, writing data, and then closing the file. Python provides several modes for file handling, including:

- `"w"`: Write mode (creates a new file or overwrites an existing file).
- `"a"`: Append mode (adds content to an existing file).
- `"x"`: Exclusive creation mode (fails if the file already exists).

1. Writing to a Text File

To write text to a file, use the `open ()` function with the `"w"` mode. Here's an example:

python

```
# Open the file for writing
with open("output.txt", "w") as file:
    file.write("Hello, World!\n")
    file.write("Welcome to Python file handling.")
```

In this example:

- "w" mode will overwrite the file if it already exists, or create a new file if it doesn't.
- file.write() writes the string to the file.

2. Writing to a CSV File

To write to a CSV file, use the csv.writer function from the csv module. Here's an example:

```python
import csv

# Data to write to the CSV file
data = [["Name", "Age"], ["Alice", 25], ["Bob", 30]]

# Open the CSV file for writing
with open("output.csv", mode="w", newline="") as file:
    csv_writer = csv.writer(file)

    # Write data to the CSV file
    csv_writer.writerows(data)
```

In this example:

- csv.writer(file) creates a writer object.
- csv_writer.writerows(data) writes multiple rows to the CSV file.

3. Writing JSON Data

To write data to a JSON file, use the json.dump() function from the json module. Here's an example:

```python
```

```python
import json

# Data to write to the JSON file
data = {"name": "Alice", "age": 25}

# Open the JSON file for writing
with open("output.json", "w") as file:
    json.dump(data, file)
```

In this example:

- `json.dump(data, file)` writes the Python dictionary `data` to a JSON file.

File Operations: Opening, Closing, and Updating Files

When working with files, it's essential to understand how to open, close, and update files correctly. Improper file handling can lead to data loss, errors, and resource leaks.

1. Opening Files

To open a file, use the `open()` function, which takes the file path and mode as arguments. The available modes are:

- `"r"`: Read mode (default mode for reading).
- `"w"`: Write mode (creates or overwrites the file).
- `"a"`: Append mode (adds to an existing file).
- `"x"`: Exclusive mode (raises an error if the file exists).

2. Closing Files

After finishing your operations with a file, it's important to **close** it using the `close()` method. This ensures that all changes are saved, and system resources are freed.

```python
file = open("sample.txt", "r")
content = file.read()
file.close()
```

Using the `with` statement automatically closes the file when you're done, making it a safer and cleaner option:

```python
with open("sample.txt", "r") as file:
    content = file.read()
```

3. Updating Files

To update a file (i.e., add or modify its contents), you can open it in "r+" (read/write) mode. This allows both reading and writing to the file.

```python
with open("sample.txt", "r+") as file:
    content = file.read()
    file.seek(0)   # Move the cursor back to the
beginning of the file
    file.write("Updated content\n")   # Overwrites the
content from the beginning
```

If you want to append to the file (i.e., add data to the end without overwriting existing content), use "a" mode.

```python
with open("sample.txt", "a") as file:
    file.write("Appended data\n")
```

Project: Build a CSV Expense Tracker

In this project, we will build a simple **CSV expense tracker** that allows users to add, view, and delete expense records.

1. Initial Setup

Create a CSV file to store the expenses. The columns will include:

- **Date**: The date the expense was recorded.
- **Description**: A short description of the expense.
- **Amount**: The amount spent.

python

```python
import csv

def create_csv_file():
    with open("expenses.csv", mode="w", newline="") as file:
        csv_writer = csv.writer(file)
        csv_writer.writerow(["Date", "Description", "Amount"])  # Writing the header
```

2. Adding an Expense

To add an expense, we will define a function that takes the date, description, and amount as inputs and writes them to the CSV file.

python

```python
def add_expense(date, description, amount):
    with open("expenses.csv", mode="a", newline="") as file:
        csv_writer = csv.writer(file)
        csv_writer.writerow([date, description, amount])
```

3. Viewing Expenses

To view the list of expenses, we will read the CSV file and display each entry.

python

```
def view_expenses():
    with open("expenses.csv", mode="r") as file:
        csv_reader = csv.reader(file)
        next(csv_reader)  # Skip the header row
        for row in csv_reader:
            print(f"Date: {row[0]}, Description:
{row[1]}, Amount: {row[2]}")
```

4. Deleting an Expense

To delete an expense, we need to read all expenses into memory, remove the specified expense, and then rewrite the remaining expenses back to the CSV file.

python

```
def delete_expense(date, description):
    expenses = []
    with open("expenses.csv", mode="r") as file:
        csv_reader = csv.reader(file)
        for row in csv_reader:
            if row[0] != date or row[1] !=
description:
                expenses.append(row)

    with open("expenses.csv", mode="w", newline="")
as file:
        csv_writer = csv.writer(file)
        csv_writer.writerows(expenses)
```

5. Running the Tracker

Finally, we will create a simple user interface that allows the user to interact with the expense tracker.

```python
python

def main():
    while True:
        print("1. Add Expense")
        print("2. View Expenses")
        print("3. Delete Expense")
        print("4. Exit")
        choice = input("Enter your choice: ")

        if choice == "1":
            date = input("Enter the date (YYYY-MM-
DD): ")
            description = input("Enter the
description: ")
            amount = input("Enter the amount: ")
            add_expense(date, description, amount)
        elif choice == "2":
            view_expenses()
        elif choice == "3":
            date = input("Enter the date of the
expense to delete: ")
            description = input("Enter the
description of the expense to delete: ")
            delete_expense(date, description)
        elif choice == "4":
            break
        else:
            print("Invalid choice. Please try
again.")
```

Understanding File Paths and Handling Directories

When working with files, it's crucial to understand how **file paths** work. A file path specifies the location of a file on the system. Paths can be either **absolute** or **relative**.

1. Absolute vs. Relative Paths

- **Absolute Path**: The full path from the root directory to the file. For example, on a Windows system:

```kotlin
C:\Users\John\Documents\project\data.txt
```

- **Relative Path**: The path relative to the current working directory. For example, if your current directory is `/home/user/project/`, a relative path to a file in a subfolder might look like:

```kotlin
data/files/data.txt
```

2. Using Python's os Module

Python provides the `os` module to interact with the operating system and handle file paths.

```python
import os

# Get the current working directory
current_directory = os.getcwd()
print(current_directory)

# Join paths
full_path = os.path.join(current_directory, "data",
"data.txt")
print(full_path)
```

3. Handling Directories

Python's `os` module also allows you to work with directories. For example, you can check if a directory exists, create a new directory, or list all files in a directory.

```python
python

# Check if a directory exists
if not os.path.exists("new_directory"):
    os.mkdir("new_directory")

# List files in a directory
files = os.listdir("data")
print(files)
```

Conclusion

In this chapter, we explored the fundamentals of working with files in Python. We learned how to read and write data to .txt, .csv, and .json files. We also built a practical CSV expense tracker application to practice these concepts.

Additionally, we discussed file operations like opening, closing, and updating files, and learned how to handle file paths and directories efficiently. Mastering file handling is essential for working with persistent data in any Python application, and the skills you've learned in this chapter will serve as a foundation for more advanced topics.

Chapter 8: Introduction to Object-Oriented Programming (OOP)

Introduction to Object-Oriented Programming (OOP)

Object-Oriented Programming (OOP) is a powerful programming paradigm that is widely used in modern software development. It allows developers to structure code in a way that is more intuitive, reusable, and scalable. Understanding OOP is essential for any developer, as it forms the backbone of many programming languages, including Python.

In traditional programming, data and functions are kept separate. This often leads to code that is hard to manage, extend, and reuse. OOP, on the other hand, organizes software design around objects and classes. These objects are self-contained units that contain both data (known as attributes) and functions (known as methods) that manipulate that data.

The main goals of OOP are to:

1. **Encapsulate**: Keep data safe and restrict direct access.
2. **Reuse**: Use existing classes and objects in new programs.
3. **Simplify**: Break down complex systems into manageable, logical chunks.

In this chapter, we will explore the fundamentals of OOP, starting with the basic concepts of **classes** and **objects**. We will then move on to **attributes** and **methods**, and we'll dive into more advanced topics like **encapsulation**, **inheritance**, and **polymorphism**.

Finally, we'll apply these concepts by designing a **Bank Account class** that demonstrates how OOP works in a real-world scenario.

What is OOP and Why is it Important?

Object-Oriented Programming is a paradigm that organizes software design around **objects**. An **object** is a self-contained unit that holds both data and the methods that operate on the data. OOP allows for creating **classes**, which are blueprints or templates for creating objects.

The Importance of OOP

OOP brings a range of benefits to software development, especially when working on large or complex systems. Here are some key reasons why OOP is important:

1. **Modularity**: By using classes, you can break down a complex system into smaller, manageable pieces. Each class encapsulates a specific part of the program, making it easier to understand and modify.
2. **Reusability**: Classes can be reused across multiple projects. Once you define a class, you can create as many objects of that class as you need without rewriting code.
3. **Maintainability**: OOP makes it easier to maintain code. Since classes are modular, fixing a bug in one class doesn't affect the rest of the program. This leads to better code organization and simpler debugging.
4. **Abstraction**: OOP allows you to hide implementation details and expose only the necessary parts of the class, which makes working with complex systems much easier.
5. **Scalability**: As your codebase grows, OOP helps you manage and scale the project by adding new classes or modifying existing ones without breaking the overall system.

Classes and Objects: Basic Structure

At the core of OOP are **classes** and **objects**. Let's start by understanding these two concepts in detail.

1. Classes: The Blueprint

A **class** is essentially a blueprint for creating objects. It defines the attributes (data) and methods (functions) that the objects created from the class will have.

In Python, a class is defined using the `class` keyword:

python

```
class Dog:
    pass
```

In this example, `Dog` is a class. Right now, it doesn't contain any attributes or methods, but we'll build on it shortly.

2. Objects: Instances of Classes

An **object** is an instance of a class. When you create an object, you are essentially creating a of the class with its own set of attributes and methods. The object can then interact with other objects and the program itself.

To create an object, you simply call the class name as if it were a function:

python

```
dog1 = Dog()  # Creating an object of the Dog class
```

Now `dog1` is an object (or instance) of the `Dog` class. The object will have all the attributes and methods defined by the class, but we'll need to define them next.

Attributes and Methods

1. Attributes: Data Stored in an Object

Attributes are variables that store data specific to an object. In the case of a `Dog` class, attributes could be things like `name`, `age`, and `breed`.

To define attributes in a class, we use the `__init__()` method, which is the constructor. It initializes the attributes when the object is created.

python

```
class Dog:
    def __init__(self, name, age, breed):
        self.name = name   # Attribute
        self.age = age     # Attribute
        self.breed = breed  # Attribute
```

In this code:

- The `__init__()` method initializes the object with the provided values (`name`, `age`, and `breed`).
- The `self` keyword refers to the current object being created. Each object has its own `name`, `age`, and `breed` attributes.

Now, you can create an object and assign values to these attributes:

python

```
dog1 = Dog("Buddy", 5, "Golden Retriever")
print(dog1.name)   # Outputs: Buddy
```

```
print(dog1.age)     # Outputs: 5
print(dog1.breed)   # Outputs: Golden Retriever
```

2. Methods: Functions Inside a Class

Methods are functions that belong to a class and can be called on an object of that class. Methods usually operate on the data stored in the attributes of the class.

Here's an example where we add a method to the `Dog` class that allows the dog to bark:

python

```python
class Dog:
    def __init__(self, name, age, breed):
        self.name = name
        self.age = age
        self.breed = breed

    def bark(self):   # Method
        print(f"{self.name} says woof!")
```

Now, we can create a `Dog` object and call the `bark()` method:

python

```python
dog1 = Dog("Buddy", 5, "Golden Retriever")
dog1.bark()   # Outputs: Buddy says woof!
```

Methods can also take arguments, just like regular functions:

python

```python
class Dog:
    def __init__(self, name, age, breed):
        self.name = name
        self.age = age
        self.breed = breed

    def greet(self, other_dog):
```

```
        print(f"{self.name} says hello to
{other_dog.name}")
```

This method accepts another `Dog` object as an argument and prints a greeting.

python

```
dog1 = Dog("Buddy", 5, "Golden Retriever")
dog2 = Dog("Max", 3, "Labrador")
dog1.greet(dog2)  # Outputs: Buddy says hello to Max
```

Project: Design a Bank Account Class

Now that we understand the basics of classes, objects, attributes, and methods, let's design a **Bank Account class**. This will allow us to practice the concepts we've learned so far.

1. Defining the Bank Account Class

We'll define a `BankAccount` class with the following features:

- **Attributes:**
  - `account_holder`: The name of the account holder.
  - `balance`: The current balance in the account.
- **Methods:**
  - `deposit()`: Adds money to the account balance.
  - `withdraw()`: Subtracts money from the account balance.
  - `display_balance()`: Displays the current balance.

python

```
class BankAccount:
    def __init__(self, account_holder, balance=0):
        self.account_holder = account_holder
        self.balance = balance
```

```
    def deposit(self, amount):
        if amount > 0:
            self.balance += amount
            print(f"Deposited {amount}. New balance:
{self.balance}")
        else:
            print("Deposit amount must be positive.")

    def withdraw(self, amount):
        if 0 < amount <= self.balance:
            self.balance -= amount
            print(f"Withdrew {amount}. New balance:
{self.balance}")
        else:
            print("Insufficient funds or invalid
amount.")

    def display_balance(self):
        print(f"Balance: {self.balance}")
```

2. Creating and Using Bank Account Objects

Now, let's create a `BankAccount` object and test the `deposit()`, `withdraw()`, and `display_balance()` methods.

python

```
account = BankAccount("Alice", 1000)
account.display_balance()  # Outputs: Balance: 1000
account.deposit(500)  # Outputs: Deposited 500. New
balance: 1500
account.withdraw(200)  # Outputs: Withdrew 200. New
balance: 1300
account.display_balance()  # Outputs: Balance: 1300
```

In this example:

- We created a `BankAccount` object with an initial balance of 1000.
- We used the `deposit()` method to add 500 to the balance.
- We used the `withdraw()` method to subtract 200 from the balance.

- We used `display_balance()` to show the current balance.

Understanding Encapsulation, Inheritance, and Polymorphism

The core principles of OOP—**encapsulation**, **inheritance**, and **polymorphism**—make code more flexible, reusable, and easier to maintain. Let's explore each of these principles in detail.

1. Encapsulation: Protecting Data

Encapsulation is the practice of hiding an object's internal state and requiring all interaction to be done through methods. This prevents external code from directly modifying the object's data and helps maintain the integrity of the object.

In Python, encapsulation is achieved by using private and public attributes. Private attributes are prefixed with an underscore _ or double underscore __ to indicate they should not be accessed directly.

python

```python
class BankAccount:
    def __init__(self, account_holder, balance=0):
        self.account_holder = account_holder
        self.__balance = balance   # Private attribute

    def deposit(self, amount):
        if amount > 0:
            self.__balance += amount

    def withdraw(self, amount):
        if 0 < amount <= self.__balance:
            self.__balance -= amount

    def display_balance(self):
```

```
    print(f"Balance: {self.__balance}")
```

In this case, the __balance attribute is private, and it can only be modified or accessed using methods. Direct access to __balance would raise an error:

python

```
account = BankAccount("Alice", 1000)
print(account.__balance)  # Raises an AttributeError
```

To interact with the private attribute, we use public methods like deposit(), withdraw(), and display_balance().

2. Inheritance: Reusing Code

Inheritance allows a class to inherit attributes and methods from another class. This makes it possible to reuse code and create new classes that are based on existing ones.

For example, let's create a SavingsAccount class that inherits from the BankAccount class:

python

```
class SavingsAccount(BankAccount):
    def __init__(self, account_holder, balance=0,
interest_rate=0.02):
        super().__init__(account_holder, balance)  #
Inherit from BankAccount
        self.interest_rate = interest_rate

    def apply_interest(self):
        interest = self.balance * self.interest_rate
        self.balance += interest
        print(f"Applied interest: {interest}. New
balance: {self.balance}")
```

In this example:

- SavingsAccount inherits from BankAccount, so it has the same attributes and methods.
- We added a new method apply_interest() to the SavingsAccount class, which calculates and adds interest to the balance.

3. Polymorphism: Using the Same Interface

Polymorphism allows different classes to provide their own implementation of a method while sharing the same interface. This is useful when you want to write code that can work with objects of different types but use the same method names.

For example, we can define a CheckingAccount class that overrides the withdraw() method to impose a fee on withdrawals:

python

```
class CheckingAccount(BankAccount):
    def __init__(self, account_holder, balance=0,
fee=2.5):
        super().__init__(account_holder, balance)
        self.fee = fee

    def withdraw(self, amount):
        if amount + self.fee <= self.balance:
            self.balance -= (amount + self.fee)
            print(f"Withdrew {amount} with a fee of
{self.fee}. New balance: {self.balance}")
        else:
            print("Insufficient funds.")
```

Here, both SavingsAccount and CheckingAccount inherit from BankAccount but implement their own version of apply_interest() and withdraw(), respectively. This is an example of polymorphism, where different classes share the same interface but have their own implementations.

Conclusion

In this chapter, we introduced the fundamental concepts of Object-Oriented Programming (OOP), including **classes**, **objects**, **attributes**, and **methods**. We also explored the core principles of OOP—**encapsulation**, **inheritance**, and **polymorphism**—and applied them to a real-world project, the **Bank Account class**.

By mastering these concepts, you can write more modular, reusable, and maintainable code. OOP is an essential skill for any developer, and understanding these principles will allow you to create more powerful, flexible applications.

Chapter 9: Advanced OOP Concepts

Introduction to Advanced OOP Concepts

In the previous chapters, we explored the basics of Object-Oriented Programming (OOP) and learned how to define classes, create objects, and use attributes and methods. However, OOP also includes some more advanced concepts that allow us to write cleaner, more efficient, and scalable code. These concepts include **inheritance**, **polymorphism**, **abstract classes**, and **interfaces**. In this chapter, we will dive into these advanced features of Python's OOP system.

By mastering these advanced OOP concepts, you can:

1. Build flexible and reusable code using **inheritance**.
2. Handle complex scenarios efficiently with **polymorphism**.
3. Define **abstract classes** and **interfaces** to create a consistent structure for your programs.
4. Learn how to apply these concepts in real-world projects, such as a **Library Management System**.

Let's break down each of these topics in detail and build a project to apply everything we've learned.

Working with Inheritance and Super

What is Inheritance?

Inheritance is a fundamental concept in OOP that allows one class (the **child** or **subclass**) to inherit attributes and methods from another class (the **parent** or **superclass**). The subclass can extend or modify the behavior of the parent class, enabling you to create new classes based on existing ones. This helps to avoid code duplication, promotes code reusability, and facilitates the maintenance of code.

Basic Syntax of Inheritance

To define a subclass that inherits from a parent class, you simply specify the parent class in parentheses after the subclass name:

python

```python
class Parent:
    def __init__(self, name):
        self.name = name

    def greet(self):
        print(f"Hello, {self.name}!")

class Child(Parent):
    def __init__(self, name, age):
        super().__init__(name)   # Call the parent
class's constructor
        self.age = age

    def introduce(self):
        print(f"I am {self.name}, and I am {self.age}
years old.")
```

In this example:

- Child is a subclass of Parent.
- The Child class inherits the __init__ and greet methods from Parent.
- The super().__init__(name) call in the Child class invokes the constructor of the parent class (Parent), allowing the Child class to initialize the name attribute from the parent class.

Using `super()` to Call the Parent Class

The `super()` function allows the subclass to call methods from the parent class. It is often used in the constructor to initialize attributes from the parent class, as demonstrated in the example above.

The `super()` function is especially useful when dealing with **multiple inheritance** (where a class inherits from more than one parent class), ensuring that all parent classes are properly initialized.

python

```
class Parent:
    def __init__(self, name):
        self.name = name

class Child(Parent):
    def __init__(self, name, age):
        super().__init__(name)   # Call the parent
constructor
        self.age = age
```

In this case, `super().__init__(name)` ensures that the `name` attribute is initialized using the `Parent` class's constructor.

Using Polymorphism for Flexibility

What is Polymorphism?

Polymorphism is the ability of different classes to provide their own implementation of a method that is defined in a common interface or base class. This allows different objects to respond to the same method call in different ways. Polymorphism enhances flexibility by enabling the same function to work with objects of different types.

Example of Polymorphism

Let's consider a scenario with a Book class and two subclasses: FictionBook and NonFictionBook. Both subclasses will inherit from Book and override the get_details method to provide specific details about the book type.

python

```python
class Book:
    def __init__(self, title, author):
        self.title = title
        self.author = author

    def get_details(self):
        return f"Title: {self.title}, Author:
{self.author}"

class FictionBook(Book):
    def get_details(self):
        return f"Fiction Book - Title: {self.title},
Author: {self.author}"

class NonFictionBook(Book):
    def get_details(self):
        return f"Non-Fiction Book - Title:
{self.title}, Author: {self.author}"

# Polymorphism in action
def print_book_details(book):
    print(book.get_details())

fiction = FictionBook("The Great Gatsby", "F. Scott
Fitzgerald")
non_fiction = NonFictionBook("Sapiens", "Yuval Noah
Harari")

print_book_details(fiction)   # Outputs: Fiction Book
- Title: The Great Gatsby, Author: F. Scott
Fitzgerald
print_book_details(non_fiction)   # Outputs: Non-
Fiction Book - Title: Sapiens, Author: Yuval Noah
Harari
```

In this example:

- Both `FictionBook` and `NonFictionBook` override the `get_details` method from the `Book` class.
- The `print_book_details` function demonstrates **polymorphism** by accepting both `FictionBook` and `NonFictionBook` objects, even though their `get_details` methods are different.

Why is Polymorphism Important?

Polymorphism makes it easier to write flexible and reusable code. Instead of writing multiple versions of the same function for different object types, you can write a single function that works with any object that implements the required method. This reduces code duplication and simplifies maintenance.

Abstract Classes and Interfaces

What is an Abstract Class?

An **abstract class** is a class that cannot be instantiated on its own. Instead, it serves as a blueprint for other classes. Abstract classes are used to define methods that must be implemented by subclasses, but they provide a common interface for all subclasses.

In Python, an abstract class is defined using the `abc` (Abstract Base Class) module. The `ABC` class and the `abstractmethod` decorator are used to define abstract classes and methods.

Example of an Abstract Class
python

```
from abc import ABC, abstractmethod

class Book(ABC):
```

```
    def __init__(self, title, author):
        self.title = title
        self.author = author

    @abstractmethod
    def get_details(self):
        pass

class FictionBook(Book):
    def get_details(self):
        return f"Fiction Book - Title: {self.title},
Author: {self.author}"

class NonFictionBook(Book):
    def get_details(self):
        return f"Non-Fiction Book - Title:
{self.title}, Author: {self.author}"

# Attempting to create an instance of Book will raise
an error
# book = Book("Generic Title", "Generic Author")  #
Raises TypeError: Can't instantiate abstract class
Book with abstract method get_details

fiction = FictionBook("1984", "George Orwell")
non_fiction = NonFictionBook("The Selfish Gene",
"Richard Dawkins")
print(fiction.get_details())  # Outputs: Fiction Book
- Title: 1984, Author: George Orwell
```

In this example:

- The `Book` class is abstract and cannot be instantiated.
- The `get_details` method is abstract, meaning that any subclass must implement this method.
- The `FictionBook` and `NonFictionBook` classes implement the `get_details` method.

What is an Interface?

An **interface** in OOP is a contract that defines a set of methods that a class must implement. Unlike abstract classes, interfaces do not contain any implementation—they only define method signatures. Python does not have a built-in interface mechanism, but you can achieve similar functionality using abstract classes.

Python uses abstract classes to simulate interfaces by defining methods without implementation, ensuring that subclasses must implement these methods.

Project: Build a Library Management System

Now that we've covered the core advanced OOP concepts, let's build a **Library Management System** using inheritance, polymorphism, and abstract classes. This system will manage different types of books, customers, and staff members.

1. Defining the Abstract Classes

We'll start by defining an abstract class `LibraryMember`, which will serve as a blueprint for both customers and staff. This class will contain abstract methods that must be implemented by its subclasses.

python

```python
from abc import ABC, abstractmethod

class LibraryMember(ABC):
    def __init__(self, name, membership_id):
        self.name = name
        self.membership_id = membership_id

    @abstractmethod
```

```python
def get_details(self):
    pass
```

2. Creating Subclasses for Customers and Staff

Now, we'll create two subclasses: `Customer` and `Staff`. These subclasses will inherit from `LibraryMember` and implement the `get_details()` method.

python

```python
class Customer(LibraryMember):
    def __init__(self, name, membership_id, borrowed_books):
        super().__init__(name, membership_id)
        self.borrowed_books = borrowed_books

    def get_details(self):
        return f"Customer Name: {self.name}, Membership ID: {self.membership_id}, Borrowed Books: {self.borrowed_books}"

class Staff(LibraryMember):
    def __init__(self, name, membership_id, role):
        super().__init__(name, membership_id)
        self.role = role

    def get_details(self):
        return f"Staff Name: {self.name}, Membership ID: {self.membership_id}, Role: {self.role}"
```

3. Working with Books and Polymorphism

We'll define a `Book` class with different types of books. Each book type will have its own implementation of the `get_details()` method, demonstrating **polymorphism**.

python

```python
class Book(ABC):
    def __init__(self, title, author):
        self.title = title
        self.author = author
```

```
    @abstractmethod
    def get_details(self):
        pass

class FictionBook(Book):
    def get_details(self):
        return f"Fiction Book - Title: {self.title},
Author: {self.author}"

class NonFictionBook(Book):
    def get_details(self):
        return f"Non-Fiction Book - Title:
{self.title}, Author: {self.author}"
```

4. Managing Library Operations

We'll now define a `Library` class that manages the books, customers, and staff. It will have methods for adding books, viewing books, and printing details of library members.

python

```python
class Library:
    def __init__(self):
        self.books = []
        self.members = []

    def add_book(self, book):
        self.books.append(book)

    def add_member(self, member):
        self.members.append(member)

    def display_books(self):
        for book in self.books:
            print(book.get_details())

    def display_members(self):
        for member in self.members:
            print(member.get_details())
```

5. Running the Library System

Now, let's put everything together by creating some books, customers, and staff members, and adding them to the library.

python

```python
# Create books
book1 = FictionBook("1984", "George Orwell")
book2 = NonFictionBook("Sapiens", "Yuval Noah
Harari")

# Create library members
customer1 = Customer("Alice", "C001", [book1])
staff1 = Staff("Bob", "S001", "Manager")

# Create library and add books and members
library = Library()
library.add_book(book1)
library.add_book(book2)
library.add_member(customer1)
library.add_member(staff1)

# Display books and members
print("Books in the Library:")
library.display_books()

print("\nLibrary Members:")
library.display_members()
```

Tips for Mastering OOP in Python

Mastering OOP requires both understanding the theory and applying it in practice. Here are some tips to help you become an expert in OOP:

1. **Practice by Building Projects**: The best way to master OOP is by building real-world projects, like a library management system or a bank account system. The more you work with

classes, objects, and inheritance, the more comfortable you'll become.

2. **Understand the Principles of OOP**: Focus on the core principles—**encapsulation**, **inheritance**, **polymorphism**, and **abstraction**. Understanding these concepts will allow you to write clean, maintainable, and reusable code.

3. **Use Inheritance Thoughtfully**: Inheritance is a powerful tool, but use it wisely. Avoid excessive inheritance chains, and instead, think about whether composition (using objects within objects) might be a better solution.

4. **Embrace Polymorphism**: Polymorphism makes your code flexible and reusable. Use it to handle different types of objects with the same method name.

5. **Leverage Abstract Classes and Interfaces**: Abstract classes help create a blueprint for your subclasses, ensuring that they implement necessary methods. Use them to enforce a consistent structure.

Conclusion

In this chapter, we covered advanced OOP concepts, including inheritance, polymorphism, abstract classes, and interfaces. We applied these concepts to build a **Library Management System**, demonstrating how inheritance and polymorphism make the system more flexible and maintainable.

Mastering these advanced OOP techniques is essential for building complex applications and writing scalable, maintainable code. By continuing to practice these concepts and working on real-world projects, you'll become proficient in object-oriented programming and ready to tackle more sophisticated challenges in your programming career.

Chapter 10: Libraries and Modules: Python Ecosystem

Introduction to Libraries and Modules in Python

Python's ecosystem is vast and rich, thanks in large part to its extensive collection of libraries and modules. Whether you're working with data, building web applications, or automating tasks, Python libraries offer powerful solutions that can make your job easier and more efficient.

In this chapter, we will explore:

1. **What Python libraries are** and why they are important.
2. **Python's standard library,** which comes bundled with Python and provides a wealth of built-in functionality.
3. **Installing and using external libraries** via `pip`, Python's package manager.
4. **Popular libraries** such as **NumPy, pandas,** and **Matplotlib,** which are essential for data science, numerical computing, and visualization.
5. A **project** that demonstrates how to use pandas to analyze data from a CSV file.
6. **Best practices** for using libraries in Python, helping you maintain clean and efficient code.

By the end of this chapter, you will have a solid understanding of how to harness the power of Python libraries to solve real-world problems.

What Are Python Libraries?

A **library** in Python is a collection of pre-written code that you can use to perform common tasks without having to write everything from scratch. Libraries in Python provide functionality for a wide range of applications, from scientific computing to web development and machine learning.

There are two types of libraries in Python:

1. **Standard Library**: A collection of modules that come with Python, which means you don't need to install anything extra to use them. The standard library includes modules for handling file I/O, data manipulation, math operations, regular expressions, networking, and more.
2. **External Libraries**: These are third-party libraries that you install separately. Many of these libraries are developed by the Python community and provide powerful tools for specialized tasks, such as data analysis (e.g., pandas), numerical computation (e.g., NumPy), and data visualization (e.g., Matplotlib).

Why Are Libraries Important?

Libraries are essential because they:

- **Save time and effort**: Instead of writing code to solve common problems, you can use an existing library.
- **Ensure consistency**: Libraries are often well-tested and follow best practices, ensuring that your code is more reliable.
- **Simplify complex tasks**: Many libraries abstract complex functionality into simple interfaces, making it easy to implement advanced features.
- **Encourage collaboration**: With libraries, you can easily share your code with others and use code written by others.

By using libraries, you can focus on solving the core problems of your application instead of reinventing the wheel.

Introduction to Python's Standard Library

Python's **standard library** is one of its greatest strengths. It comes bundled with Python, so there's no need to install anything extra to start using it. The standard library covers a wide variety of functionality, from working with data structures to interacting with the operating system.

Key Modules in the Standard Library

Here are some of the most commonly used modules in the standard library:

1. **os**: Provides functions for interacting with the operating system, such as working with file paths, directories, and environment variables.

    python

    ```python
    import os
    print(os.getcwd())  # Get the current working
    directory
    ```

2. **math**: Offers mathematical functions like trigonometric operations, logarithms, and constants (e.g., pi).

    python

    ```python
    import math
    print(math.sqrt(16))  # Outputs: 4.0
    ```

3. **datetime**: Used for working with dates and times.

```python
python

import datetime
now = datetime.datetime.now()
print(now)   # Outputs the current date and time
```

4. **json**: Provides functions for working with JSON data (e.g., loading JSON from a string or writing JSON to a file).

```python
python

import json
data = {"name": "Alice", "age": 25}
json_data = json.dumps(data)
print(json_data)   # Outputs: {"name": "Alice",
"age": 25}
```

5. **random**: Used to generate random numbers or make random selections from a list.

```python
python

import random
print(random.randint(1, 100))   # Outputs a
random integer between 1 and 100
```

The standard library is an extensive collection, and exploring it can significantly speed up development by reducing the need for external dependencies.

Installing External Libraries with pip

Python's package manager, **pip**, allows you to install and manage external libraries. Most external libraries are hosted on the **Python Package Index (PyPI)**, which is the official repository for Python packages.

Installing External Libraries

To install a library using `pip`, you simply need to run the following command in your terminal or command prompt:

```bash
pip install library_name
```

For example, to install **pandas** (a popular library for data analysis), run:

```bash
pip install pandas
```

After installation, you can import the library into your Python script:

```python
import pandas as pd
```

Managing Installed Libraries

You can list all the installed libraries in your environment with the following command:

```bash
pip list
```

If you want to update a library to the latest version, you can use:

```bash
pip install --upgrade library_name
```

To uninstall a library, you can use:

```bash
```

```
pip uninstall library_name
```

Using Virtual Environments

It's best practice to use **virtual environments** to manage project-specific dependencies. A virtual environment is a self-contained directory that contains the Python interpreter and all the libraries for a specific project, preventing conflicts between different projects.

You can create a virtual environment using `venv` (included in Python's standard library):

bash

```
python -m venv myenv
```

To activate the virtual environment, run:

- On Windows:

    bash

    ```
    myenv\Scripts\activate
    ```

- On macOS/Linux:

    bash

    ```
    source myenv/bin/activate
    ```

Once activated, you can install libraries into the virtual environment using `pip`.

Popular Libraries: NumPy, pandas, and Matplotlib

Let's take a closer look at three of the most popular external libraries in Python: **NumPy**, **pandas**, and **Matplotlib**. These libraries are widely used in data science and scientific computing.

1. NumPy: Numerical Computing

NumPy is the foundation of numerical computing in Python. It provides support for **arrays** (multi-dimensional matrices), and mathematical operations that are efficient and fast.

- **Creating a NumPy Array**

python

```python
import numpy as np
arr = np.array([1, 2, 3, 4])
print(arr)  # Outputs: [1 2 3 4]
```

- **Array Operations**

NumPy arrays support element-wise operations, such as addition, multiplication, and trigonometric functions.

python

```python
arr1 = np.array([1, 2, 3])
arr2 = np.array([4, 5, 6])

# Element-wise addition
result = arr1 + arr2
print(result)  # Outputs: [5 7 9]
```

- **Multi-Dimensional Arrays**

```python
python
```

```python
arr = np.array([[1, 2], [3, 4], [5, 6]])
print(arr.shape)  # Outputs: (3, 2)
```

NumPy is especially useful for large datasets and performing operations on matrices, which are common in machine learning and data science.

2. pandas: Data Analysis

pandas is a powerful library used for data manipulation and analysis. It provides two main data structures: **Series** (1D data) and **DataFrame** (2D data).

- **Creating a DataFrame**

```python
python
```

```python
import pandas as pd

data = {'Name': ['Alice', 'Bob', 'Charlie'], 'Age':
[25, 30, 35]}
df = pd.DataFrame(data)
print(df)
```

This creates a simple DataFrame:

```markdown
markdown
```

```
     Name  Age
0    Alice   25
1      Bob   30
2  Charlie   35
```

- **DataFrame Operations**

You can easily filter, sort, and manipulate data with pandas.

```
python
```

```python
# Filter rows where age is greater than 30
filtered_df = df[df['Age'] > 30]
print(filtered_df)
```

- **Reading and Writing CSV Files**

```
python
```

```python
# Reading a CSV file into a DataFrame
df = pd.read_csv('data.csv')

# Writing a DataFrame to a CSV file
df.to_csv('output.csv', index=False)
```

pandas is a go-to library for anyone working with tabular data, as it provides intuitive methods for manipulating, cleaning, and analyzing large datasets.

3. Matplotlib: Data Visualization

Matplotlib is a library for creating static, animated, and interactive visualizations in Python. It's widely used for plotting graphs and charts.

- **Basic Plotting**

```
python
```

```python
import matplotlib.pyplot as plt

x = [1, 2, 3, 4, 5]
y = [2, 4, 6, 8, 10]

plt.plot(x, y)
plt.xlabel('X-axis')
plt.ylabel('Y-axis')
plt.title('Basic Plot')
plt.show()
```

This simple code plots a line graph with labeled axes.

- **Creating a Bar Chart**

```python
categories = ['A', 'B', 'C']
values = [10, 20, 30]

plt.bar(categories, values)
plt.title('Bar Chart')
plt.show()
```

Matplotlib allows you to create a wide range of visualizations, from line plots and bar charts to histograms and scatter plots, making it an essential tool for data analysis and presentation.

Project: Analyze Data from a CSV File with pandas

Let's build a small project that demonstrates how to use **pandas** to analyze data stored in a CSV file. In this project, we will:

1. Read the data from a CSV file.
2. Perform some basic data analysis.
3. Generate insights and summaries from the data.

Step 1: Prepare the CSV Data

Imagine we have a CSV file called `sales_data.csv` with the following content:

```mathematica
Date,Product,Units Sold,Revenue
2023-01-01,Product A,100,5000
2023-01-02,Product B,150,7500
2023-01-03,Product A,200,10000
2023-01-04,Product C,50,2500
```

Step 2: Load the Data with pandas

First, we will read the CSV file into a pandas DataFrame.

```python
import pandas as pd

# Load the CSV file into a DataFrame
df = pd.read_csv('sales_data.csv')
print(df)
```

This will display the content of the CSV file as a DataFrame:

```yaml
         Date    Product  Units Sold  Revenue
0  2023-01-01  Product A         100     5000
1  2023-01-02  Product B         150     7500
2  2023-01-03  Product A         200    10000
3  2023-01-04  Product C          50     2500
```

Step 3: Data Analysis

Now, let's perform some basic analysis on this dataset.

- **Total Units Sold and Revenue**

python

```python
total_units_sold = df['Units Sold'].sum()
total_revenue = df['Revenue'].sum()

print(f"Total Units Sold: {total_units_sold}")
print(f"Total Revenue: ${total_revenue}")
```

- **Average Units Sold per Product**

python

```python
average_units_per_product =
df.groupby('Product')['Units Sold'].mean()
print(average_units_per_product)
```

- **Filter Data for Specific Products**

Let's filter the data to see only the sales for `Product A`.

python

```python
product_a_sales = df[df['Product'] == 'Product A']
print(product_a_sales)
```

Step 4: Data Visualization

We can also visualize the sales data using **Matplotlib**. Let's create a bar chart showing the total revenue for each product.

python

```python
import matplotlib.pyplot as plt
```

```
# Group data by product and sum the revenue
revenue_by_product =
df.groupby('Product')['Revenue'].sum()

# Plot the bar chart
revenue_by_product.plot(kind='bar', color='skyblue')
plt.title('Total Revenue by Product')
plt.xlabel('Product')
plt.ylabel('Revenue')
plt.show()
```

This will generate a bar chart that visualizes the total revenue for each product.

Best Practices for Using Libraries

While Python libraries are powerful tools that can simplify your development process, it's important to follow best practices when using them. Here are some tips for using libraries effectively:

1. Install Only What You Need

When working with external libraries, install only the libraries you need for your project. This keeps your environment clean and minimizes dependency conflicts.

bash

```
pip install pandas
```

2. Use Virtual Environments

Use virtual environments to manage your project's dependencies. This ensures that your libraries won't conflict with other projects and makes it easier to manage dependencies for different projects.

bash

```
python -m venv myenv
source myenv/bin/activate  # On macOS/Linux
myenv\Scripts\activate  # On Windows
```

3. Keep Libraries Up to Date

Ensure that you're using the latest versions of libraries to take advantage of new features, bug fixes, and performance improvements.

```
bash
```

```
pip install --upgrade pandas
```

4. Read Documentation

Before using a new library, always refer to its official documentation. This will help you understand the library's functionality, installation requirements, and how to use it efficiently.

5. Modularize Your Code

If you're using multiple libraries in your project, try to keep your code modular by grouping related functionalities together. For instance, use separate functions or classes for data manipulation, analysis, and visualization.

Conclusion

In this chapter, we explored the world of **Python libraries** and how they can significantly simplify development. We learned about the **standard library,** how to **install and use external libraries,** and delved into popular libraries like **NumPy, pandas,** and **Matplotlib.** Additionally, we worked through a project that demonstrated how to use pandas to analyze and visualize data from a CSV file.

By leveraging Python's rich ecosystem of libraries, you can accomplish complex tasks more easily and write clean, maintainable code.

Chapter 11: Building Web Applications with Flask

Introduction to Web Development with Flask

Web development has become a critical skill for any software developer, as it involves creating applications that users can interact with through a web browser. A web framework is a toolkit that helps you build web applications by providing tools and libraries to handle common tasks like routing, templating, and interacting with databases.

Flask is a lightweight web framework for Python that is designed to be simple, flexible, and easy to extend. Flask gives you the basics you need to build a web application, but it also allows you to add additional features as your application grows. Unlike heavier frameworks like Django, Flask is a microframework, meaning it focuses on simplicity and leaves most of the customization to the developer.

In this chapter, we will walk through the process of building a web application using Flask, from setting it up to building a simple blog application. Along the way, we will cover key concepts like routing, templates, and debugging common web application issues.

By the end of this chapter, you will be able to create web applications using Flask, and understand the core principles of web development.

What is Flask? Introduction to Web Frameworks

A **web framework** is a set of tools and libraries that help developers build web applications by abstracting many of the repetitive tasks involved in web development. Web frameworks handle common tasks like processing HTTP requests, interacting with databases, and rendering templates.

Flask is one of the most popular web frameworks in Python. It is designed to be lightweight and simple, but flexible enough to scale as your application grows. Flask provides only the essential components for building a web application, but it allows you to extend and customize it with additional libraries and tools as needed.

Key Features of Flask:

- **Minimalistic and Lightweight**: Flask comes with minimal built-in functionality, allowing developers to choose the tools and libraries they need.
- **Extensible**: Flask provides easy integration with external libraries for features like database interaction (SQLAlchemy), form handling (WTForms), and authentication (Flask-Login).
- **Routing**: Flask allows you to map URLs to functions, making it easy to handle different parts of your web application.
- **Template Engine**: Flask uses Jinja2, a powerful templating engine that allows you to separate HTML structure from Python code.

While Flask is simple to use and great for beginners, it is also powerful enough to build complex web applications. Whether you're creating a small personal project or a large-scale web application, Flask provides the flexibility to get the job done.

Setting Up Flask for Your First Web App

To get started with Flask, you need to set up your development environment and install the required dependencies. Below are the steps for setting up Flask and creating your first web application.

Step 1: Install Flask

First, make sure you have Python installed on your system. If you don't have Flask installed yet, you can install it using Python's package manager `pip`.

bash

```bash
pip install Flask
```

Flask will automatically install all of its dependencies, including the Jinja2 templating engine and Werkzeug, which is a utility library used for HTTP handling.

Step 2: Create a Simple Flask Application

Once Flask is installed, you can create your first Flask application. Create a new file called `app.py` in your project directory, and add the following code:

python

```python
from flask import Flask

# Create a Flask application instance
app = Flask(__name__)

# Define a route
@app.route('/')
def home():
    return "Hello, World!"

# Run the app
```

```
if __name__ == "__main__":
    app.run(debug=True)
```

In this code:

- `Flask(__name__)` creates a Flask application instance. The `__name__` argument tells Flask where to find resources and templates.
- `@app.route('/')` defines a route that maps the URL path / to the `home()` function. When users visit the root URL of the application, the `home()` function is called, returning the message `"Hello, World!"`.
- `app.run(debug=True)` starts the Flask development server with debugging enabled, so any errors will be displayed in the browser.

Step 3: Running the Flask Application

To run the Flask application, open your terminal or command prompt, navigate to the directory where `app.py` is located, and run the following command:

```bash
python app.py
```

You should see output indicating that the Flask development server is running:

```csharp
 * Running on http://127.0.0.1:5000/ (Press CTRL+C to quit)
```

Open your web browser and visit `http://127.0.0.1:5000/`. You should see the text "Hello, World!" displayed.

Routing and Templates

One of the core features of Flask is **routing,** which maps URLs to functions in your application. In this section, we will explore how to use Flask's routing system and how to work with templates to render dynamic HTML pages.

1. Routing in Flask

Routes are the URLs that users can visit to access different parts of your application. You define routes in Flask using the `@app.route()` decorator, followed by the URL path and the function that handles that route.

Here's an example of routing to multiple pages:

```python
from flask import Flask

app = Flask(__name__)

@app.route('/')
def home():
    return "Welcome to the Home Page!"

@app.route('/about')
def about():
    return "This is the About Page."

if __name__ == "__main__":
    app.run(debug=True)
```

Now, if you visit:

- `http://127.0.0.1:5000/`, you'll see the home page message.
- `http://127.0.0.1:5000/about`, you'll see the about page message.

2. Dynamic URLs with Parameters

Flask also allows you to create dynamic URLs that accept parameters. For example, you might want to show a user's profile based on their username.

python

```
@app.route('/profile/<username>')
def profile(username):
    return f"Profile page of {username}"
```

Now, if you visit `http://127.0.0.1:5000/profile/john`, it will display: `Profile page of john`.

3. Using Templates for Dynamic Content

While returning simple text from routes is useful for testing, in real-world applications, you'll often want to render HTML pages with dynamic content. Flask uses the Jinja2 template engine to do this.

First, create a directory called `templates` in your project directory. Inside this directory, create a file called `home.html` with the following content:

html

```
<!DOCTYPE html>
<html>
<head>
    <title>Welcome to Flask</title>
</head>
<body>
    <h1>{{ message }}</h1>
</body>
</html>
```

Now, update your `app.py` to render the template with dynamic content:

```python
from flask import Flask, render_template

app = Flask(__name__)

@app.route('/')
def home():
    message = "Welcome to the Flask Web Application!"
    return render_template('home.html',
message=message)

if __name__ == "__main__":
    app.run(debug=True)
```

In this code:

- `render_template('home.html', message=message)` renders the `home.html` template and passes the variable `message` to it.
- Inside the template, `{{ message }}` is replaced with the value of the `message` variable.

Now, when you visit `http://127.0.0.1:5000/`, you'll see a dynamically generated HTML page with the message "Welcome to the Flask Web Application!"

Project: Build a Simple Blog Application

Now that you understand the basics of Flask routing and templates, let's build a simple **Blog Application**. This application will allow users to:

1. View all blog posts.
2. View a single post.
3. Add a new post (using a form).
4. Delete a post.

1. Setting Up the Application

Let's start by defining a basic `BlogPost` class to represent a blog post:

python

```python
class BlogPost:
    def __init__(self, title, content):
        self.title = title
        self.content = content
```

Next, we create a list to store the blog posts:

python

```python
posts = [
    BlogPost("First Post", "This is the content of
the first post."),
    BlogPost("Second Post", "This is the content of
the second post."),
]
```

2. Routes for Viewing and Adding Posts

Let's add routes for viewing all posts and viewing a single post:

python

```python
@app.route('/')
def index():
    return render_template('index.html', posts=posts)

@app.route('/post/<int:post_id>')
def post(post_id):
    post = posts[post_id]
    return render_template('post.html', post=post)
```

3. Adding a New Post

To allow users to add a new post, we'll create a form where users can enter the title and content. First, create a route to display the form:

python

```python
@app.route('/new', methods=['GET', 'POST'])
def new_post():
    if request.method == 'POST':
        title = request.form['title']
        content = request.form['content']
        posts.append(BlogPost(title, content))
        return redirect(url_for('index'))
    return render_template('new_post.html')
```

This route will handle both displaying the form (GET request) and processing the form data (POST request).

Create a form in new_post.html:

html

```html
<form method="POST">
    <label for="title">Title</label>
    <input type="text" id="title" name="title"
required><br>

    <label for="content">Content</label>
    <textarea id="content" name="content"
required></textarea><br>

    <input type="submit" value="Add Post">
</form>
```

4. Deleting a Post

Finally, let's add a route for deleting a post:

```python
python
```

```python
@app.route('/delete/<int:post_id>')
def delete(post_id):
    posts.pop(post_id)
    return redirect(url_for('index'))
```

5. Project Structure

Your project directory should now look something like this:

```bash
bash
```

```bash
/blog
    /templates
        index.html
        post.html
        new_post.html
    app.py
```

6. Running the Blog Application

Run the application by executing `python app.py` in your terminal. Open `http://127.0.0.1:5000/` in your browser to interact with your blog.

Debugging Web Applications: Common Issues

When working with web applications, debugging is an essential skill. Web apps can encounter a variety of issues, from routing errors to template rendering problems. Here are some common issues you might encounter when developing Flask applications, and how to debug them.

1. Routing Issues

If your routes aren't working as expected (e.g., the page returns a 404 error), make sure:

- The URL path in the route is correct.
- You are using the correct HTTP methods (e.g., `GET`, `POST`).
- You've included the proper argument names in the route functions (e.g., `post_id` in the URL).

2. Template Not Found

If Flask can't find your template, check that:

- The templates are located in the `templates` folder.
- You're passing the correct variable names to `render_template()`.
- The template file extensions are correct (`.html`).

3. Form Handling Issues

When handling forms, make sure you're using `request.form` to get form data and that the form method is `POST`. Additionally, check for form validation errors or missing form fields.

```python
title = request.form['title']
content = request.form['content']
```

4. Database Issues (when applicable)

If you're working with a database and encounter issues like connection errors or missing data, make sure:

- The database is properly configured and running.
- Your queries are correct.

- You're handling exceptions (e.g., using `try`/`except` blocks) to catch database errors.

Conclusion

In this chapter, we introduced Flask and explored how to build a simple web application. We covered:

- **Setting up Flask** for web development.
- **Routing** to create dynamic URLs.
- **Templates** for rendering HTML pages with dynamic content.
- **Building a Blog Application** using Flask, which involved creating routes, handling forms, and managing blog posts.
- **Debugging common issues** that arise when building web applications.

By mastering Flask and the principles covered in this chapter, you'll be well-equipped to build dynamic and interactive web applications. In the next chapter, we will dive deeper into more advanced topics such as form validation, working with databases, and authentication. Keep practicing and exploring Flask to take your web development skills to the next level!

Chapter 12: Databases and Python: Connecting to SQLite

Introduction to Databases and SQL

A **database** is a structured collection of data that can be easily accessed, managed, and updated. Databases are used to store large amounts of information efficiently and allow users or applications to retrieve and modify this data as needed. For example, databases are used to store everything from user information and product details to financial transactions.

Databases are a fundamental part of modern software applications, especially those that require persistent storage. Without databases, data would need to be stored in files, which is inefficient and difficult to manage as the data grows in size.

In this chapter, we'll introduce the basics of databases, SQL (Structured Query Language), and specifically **SQLite**, which is a lightweight and easy-to-use database that doesn't require a separate server.

We will also learn how to connect to SQLite using Python, interact with a database, and build a practical project: a **User Registration System** that stores user data in an SQLite database.

What is a Database?

A database is a collection of organized data that can be easily accessed, managed, and updated. In simple terms, it's like a digital filing system. The data is structured in a way that makes it efficient to retrieve, manipulate, and store large amounts of information.

There are many types of databases, but they all share the common goal of storing and managing data efficiently. The most common types of databases are:

1. **Relational Databases**: These databases store data in tables with rows and columns. Each table contains data about a specific entity, and relationships between tables are established through keys. Examples of relational databases include MySQL, PostgreSQL, and SQLite.
2. **Non-Relational (NoSQL) Databases**: These databases store data in formats like key-value pairs, documents, or graphs. Examples of NoSQL databases include MongoDB and Redis.

For the purpose of this chapter, we will focus on **relational databases**, specifically **SQLite**. Relational databases are the most widely used in web development and application programming, and they offer a flexible way to organize data.

Introduction to SQL and SQLite

What is SQL?

SQL (Structured Query Language) is a standardized programming language used to manage and manipulate relational databases. SQL allows you to interact with a database by performing operations such as:

- **Creating**: Defining the structure of a database or table.
- **Reading**: Retrieving data from a database.
- **Updating**: Modifying existing data in a database.
- **Deleting**: Removing data from a database.

The four basic operations of SQL are often referred to as **CRUD**:

- **C**: Create (Insert new data)
- **R**: Read (Query data)
- **U**: Update (Modify existing data)
- **D**: Delete (Remove data)

SQL uses commands like `SELECT`, `INSERT`, `UPDATE`, and `DELETE` to interact with the database.

What is SQLite?

SQLite is a self-contained, serverless relational database engine. Unlike other relational database management systems (RDBMS), such as MySQL or PostgreSQL, SQLite does not require a separate server process. Instead, it stores data in a single file on the disk, making it ideal for small to medium-sized applications, development, or testing.

Key characteristics of SQLite include:

- **Serverless**: SQLite operates directly within the application and does not require a separate server process.
- **Zero Configuration**: SQLite is easy to set up and use; it requires no installation or configuration.
- **Lightweight**: The SQLite database engine is small and efficient, with a low memory footprint.

SQLite is widely used in applications where simplicity and portability are important, such as desktop applications, mobile apps, and small-scale web applications.

Using Python to Connect to SQLite

Python provides a built-in library called **sqlite3** for interacting with SQLite databases. This module allows Python programs to connect to an SQLite database, execute SQL queries, and manage the results.

1. Setting Up SQLite in Python

Before we start using SQLite, we need to make sure the `sqlite3` module is available. Fortunately, it comes pre-installed with Python, so there's no need to install anything.

To connect to an SQLite database, we use the `sqlite3.connect()` function, which opens a connection to the database file. If the database file does not exist, SQLite will automatically create it.

Example: Connecting to a Database
python

```python
import sqlite3

# Connect to an SQLite database (or create it if it
doesn't exist)
connection = sqlite3.connect('example.db')

# Create a cursor object to interact with the
database
cursor = connection.cursor()

# Close the connection when done
connection.close()
```

In this example:

- `sqlite3.connect('example.db')` opens the `example.db` database file (or creates it if it doesn't exist).
- `cursor = connection.cursor()` creates a cursor object that is used to execute SQL commands.
- `connection.close()` closes the database connection when you're finished.

2. Creating Tables

Before we can store data in a database, we need to create tables. A table is where the actual data will be stored in the database.

Example: Creating a Table
python

```
connection = sqlite3.connect('example.db')
cursor = connection.cursor()

# Create a table
cursor.execute('''
CREATE TABLE IF NOT EXISTS users (
    id INTEGER PRIMARY KEY AUTOINCREMENT,
    username TEXT NOT NULL,
    password TEXT NOT NULL
)
''')

# Commit the changes and close the connection
connection.commit()
connection.close()
```

In this code:

- `cursor.execute()` is used to execute an SQL command. The `CREATE TABLE` command creates a new table named `users` with three columns: `id`, `username`, and `password`.
- `PRIMARY KEY AUTOINCREMENT` makes the `id` column unique and automatically increments each time a new record is inserted.
- `NOT NULL` ensures that the `username` and `password` columns cannot be left empty.

3. Inserting Data into a Table

Once we have created a table, we can insert data into it using the `INSERT INTO` SQL command.

Example: Inserting Data
python

```
connection = sqlite3.connect('example.db')
cursor = connection.cursor()

# Insert a new user into the users table
cursor.execute('''
INSERT INTO users (username, password) VALUES (?, ?)
''', ('john_doe', 'password123'))

# Commit the changes and close the connection
connection.commit()
connection.close()
```

In this example:

- `cursor.execute()` inserts a new row into the `users` table. The `?` placeholders are used to prevent SQL injection attacks, and the actual values are passed as a tuple (`('john_doe', 'password123')`).
- `connection.commit()` commits the transaction to save the changes to the database.

4. Querying Data from the Database

To retrieve data from the database, we use the `SELECT` SQL command.

Example: Querying Data
python

```
connection = sqlite3.connect('example.db')
cursor = connection.cursor()

# Select all rows from the users table
cursor.execute('SELECT * FROM users')

# Fetch all results
rows = cursor.fetchall()
```

```
# Print each row
for row in rows:
    print(row)

# Close the connection
connection.close()
```

In this example:

- `cursor.execute('SELECT * FROM users')` retrieves all rows from the `users` table.
- `cursor.fetchall()` fetches all results as a list of tuples.
- Each row is printed to the console.

Project: Build a User Registration System with SQLite

Now that we've covered the basics of connecting to and interacting with SQLite, let's build a simple **User Registration System**. This system will allow users to register by providing their username and password, and the information will be stored in an SQLite database.

Step 1: Define the Database and Table

First, we'll create the `users` table, where user information will be stored. Each user will have an `id`, `username`, and `password`.

```python
import sqlite3

def create_table():
    connection = sqlite3.connect('users.db')
    cursor = connection.cursor()

    cursor.execute('''
```

```
CREATE TABLE IF NOT EXISTS users (
    id INTEGER PRIMARY KEY AUTOINCREMENT,
    username TEXT NOT NULL,
    password TEXT NOT NULL
)
''')

connection.commit()
connection.close()
```

create_table()

Step 2: User Registration Function

Next, we'll create a function that allows users to register. This function will accept a username and password, validate the inputs, and insert the data into the database.

python

```
def register_user(username, password):
    connection = sqlite3.connect('users.db')
    cursor = connection.cursor()

    # Check if the username already exists
    cursor.execute('SELECT * FROM users WHERE
username = ?', (username,))
    existing_user = cursor.fetchone()
    if existing_user:
        print("Username already taken.")
        return

    # Insert the new user into the database
    cursor.execute('''
    INSERT INTO users (username, password) VALUES (?,
?)
    ''', (username, password))

    connection.commit()
    connection.close()

    print("User registered successfully!")
```

```
# Example usage
register_user("john_doe", "password123")
```

In this function:

- We check if the username already exists in the database using `SELECT * FROM users WHERE username = ?`.
- If the username exists, we notify the user and return early.
- Otherwise, we insert the new user into the `users` table.

Step 3: User Login Function

We'll also create a simple login function that checks if the entered username and password match any records in the database.

```python
def login_user(username, password):
    connection = sqlite3.connect('users.db')
    cursor = connection.cursor()

    cursor.execute('SELECT * FROM users WHERE
username = ? AND password = ?', (username, password))
    user = cursor.fetchone()

    if user:
        print("Login successful!")
    else:
        print("Invalid username or password.")

    connection.close()
```

```
# Example usage
login_user("john_doe", "password123")
```

In this function:

- We query the `users` table for a record that matches both the `username` and `password`.

- If a match is found, the user is logged in successfully; otherwise, an error message is displayed.

Step 4: Putting It All Together

Finally, let's add a simple menu that allows the user to choose between registering and logging in.

python

```python
def main():
    while True:
        print("1. Register")
        print("2. Login")
        print("3. Exit")

        choice = input("Choose an option: ")

        if choice == "1":
            username = input("Enter username: ")
            password = input("Enter password: ")
            register_user(username, password)
        elif choice == "2":
            username = input("Enter username: ")
            password = input("Enter password: ")
            login_user(username, password)
        elif choice == "3":
            break
        else:
            print("Invalid option, please try
again.")

if __name__ == "__main__":
    main()
```

This menu allows the user to register or log in, depending on their choice. The program will keep running until the user chooses to exit.

Best Practices for Database Interaction

Interacting with databases is an essential part of any software application. Here are some best practices to ensure efficient, secure, and maintainable database interactions:

1. Use Parameterized Queries

Always use parameterized queries to prevent SQL injection attacks. SQL injection occurs when a malicious user can manipulate a SQL query by providing unexpected input, leading to potential security vulnerabilities.

```python
python
```

```python
cursor.execute('SELECT * FROM users WHERE username =
?', (username,))
```

By using placeholders (?), you ensure that the inputs are properly sanitized.

2. Use Context Managers for Connections

Always use context managers (i.e., `with` statements) to manage database connections. This ensures that the connection is properly closed even if an error occurs.

```python
python
```

```python
with sqlite3.connect('users.db') as connection:
    cursor = connection.cursor()
    cursor.execute('SELECT * FROM users')
```

3. Commit Changes After Data Modification

Whenever you modify data in the database (e.g., insert, update, or delete), always call `connection.commit()` to save the changes. Failing to do so may result in lost data.

4. Validate User Input

Before inserting data into the database, always validate the user input to ensure that it meets the required format and constraints (e.g., username length, password strength).

Conclusion

In this chapter, we learned how to connect to an SQLite database using Python, perform CRUD operations (Create, Read, Update, Delete), and build a **User Registration System**. We covered key concepts like:

- What a database is and how it works.
- SQL basics and how to use SQLite with Python.
- How to create tables, insert data, and query data.
- Building a simple project that implements user registration and login functionality.
- Best practices for database interactions, including parameterized queries, using context managers, and validating input.

By mastering these skills, you'll be well-equipped to build data-driven applications that rely on databases for storing and managing user information

Chapter 13: Introduction to APIs: Interfacing with the Web

What Are APIs and Why Should You Care?

In the world of software development, **APIs** (Application Programming Interfaces) are essential building blocks that allow different software applications to communicate with each other. Whether you are building a web application, working with third-party services, or integrating data from various sources, APIs provide the means to send and receive information between different systems in a structured way.

What is an API?

At its core, an **API** is a set of rules that defines how one piece of software can interact with another. APIs specify the methods and data formats that applications can use to request and exchange information.

APIs can be thought of as the "middlemen" between software systems. For example, when you use a mobile app to check the weather, that app is making a request to a weather service's API to get the data it needs, such as the current temperature, forecast, and other weather conditions.

APIs are typically divided into two types:

1. **Public APIs**: These APIs are available to developers and are designed to be used by external parties. For example, Google Maps API or Twitter API.

2. **Private APIs**: These are internal APIs used by an organization for its own services or systems.

Why Should You Care About APIs?

APIs are everywhere and are integral to modern software development. Here are a few reasons why you should care about APIs:

1. **Efficiency**: APIs allow developers to integrate functionality without having to build everything from scratch. For example, instead of developing a weather forecasting system from the ground up, you can use an API like OpenWeatherMap to access accurate and up-to-date weather data.
2. **Interoperability**: APIs allow different applications, written in different programming languages, to communicate with each other. This makes it easier to integrate with other systems, services, or data sources, regardless of the technology they use.
3. **Automation**: APIs make it easier to automate processes. For example, you can set up a script that fetches stock prices every hour using a financial data API, processes the information, and sends an alert if certain conditions are met.
4. **Access to Valuable Data**: Many online services provide APIs that offer valuable data. Whether it's weather data, social media metrics, or financial data, APIs enable developers to access this information and use it in their own applications.

In short, APIs are a crucial part of the modern web and application development ecosystem. Understanding how to work with APIs will open up new possibilities for integrating external services, automating tasks, and building more powerful applications.

Using Python's Requests Library to Work with APIs

Python is an excellent language for working with APIs, and the **Requests** library makes it easy to send HTTP requests to interact with APIs. HTTP (Hypertext Transfer Protocol) is the protocol used by the web to transfer data, and APIs often use HTTP methods like GET and POST to handle requests and responses.

1. Installing the Requests Library

The `requests` library is not included in Python's standard library, but it can be easily installed using `pip`:

bash

```
pip install requests
```

Once installed, you can import it into your Python code to start making API requests.

2. Making HTTP Requests (GET, POST)

When interacting with APIs, there are several types of HTTP requests you will commonly use:

- **GET**: Used to retrieve data from the server. This is the most common HTTP request when working with APIs.
- **POST**: Used to send data to the server. POST requests are often used when submitting data (e.g., creating a new user, sending a form, etc.).

Example: Making a GET Request

A **GET** request retrieves data from an API. Here's how you can make a simple GET request using the `requests` library:

```python
import requests

# Define the API endpoint
url = "https://jsonplaceholder.typicode.com/posts"

# Make the GET request
response = requests.get(url)

# Check if the request was successful (status code
200)
if response.status_code == 200:
    # Print the JSON response
    print(response.json())
else:
    print(f"Failed to retrieve data. Status code:
{response.status_code}")
```

In this example:

- We use the `requests.get(url)` method to send a GET request to the API.
- The response from the server is stored in the `response` object.
- We check if the request was successful by examining the status code (`200` means success).
- If successful, we use `response.json()` to parse the response body as JSON data and print it.

Example: Making a POST Request

A **POST** request sends data to an API. Here's how to send data to an API with a POST request:

```python
import requests

# Define the API endpoint
url = "https://jsonplaceholder.typicode.com/posts"
```

```
# Data to send in the request body (as a dictionary)
data = {
    "title": "foo",
    "body": "bar",
    "userId": 1
}

# Make the POST request
response = requests.post(url, json=data)

# Check if the request was successful
if response.status_code == 201:   # 201 Created
    print("Data posted successfully:",
response.json())
else:
    print(f"Failed to post data. Status code:
{response.status_code}")
```

In this example:

- We send a dictionary `data` with the required data to be posted to the API.
- The `requests.post(url, json=data)` method sends the POST request with the data.
- If the request is successful, we check for a status code of `201` (Created) and print the response.

Project: Build a Weather Forecast App Using an API

Now that you know how to make basic HTTP requests, let's apply what we've learned by building a simple **Weather Forecast Application**. In this project, we will use a public weather API (such as OpenWeatherMap or WeatherAPI) to retrieve weather data and display it to the user.

1. Setting Up the API Key

To access a weather API, you will usually need to sign up for an API key. Most weather services, like OpenWeatherMap or WeatherAPI, require you to register and get an API key, which is used to authenticate your requests.

For example, you can sign up for OpenWeatherMap's API and get an API key here: https://openweathermap.org/api.

2. Making the GET Request to the Weather API

Once you have your API key, you can use it to make requests to the API to get weather data. Here's an example of how to get the current weather for a specific city using the OpenWeatherMap API:

python

```python
import requests

# Define the API endpoint and your API key
api_key = "your_api_key_here"
city = "London"
url =
f"http://api.openweathermap.org/data/2.5/weather?q={c
ity}&appid={api_key}&units=metric"

# Make the GET request
response = requests.get(url)

# Check if the request was successful
if response.status_code == 200:
    # Parse the JSON response
    data = response.json()

    # Extract relevant data
    temperature = data['main']['temp']
    weather_description =
data['weather'][0]['description']
    humidity = data['main']['humidity']
    wind_speed = data['wind']['speed']
```

```
    # Print the weather data
    print(f"Weather in {city}:")
    print(f"Temperature: {temperature}°C")
    print(f"Description: {weather_description}")
    print(f"Humidity: {humidity}%")
    print(f"Wind Speed: {wind_speed} m/s")
else:
    print(f"Failed to retrieve weather data. Status
code: {response.status_code}")
```

In this example:

- We pass the `city` and `api_key` in the URL to make a request to the weather API.
- We extract the temperature, weather description, humidity, and wind speed from the JSON response.
- The data is then printed to the console.

3. Building a Simple Command-Line Weather App

We can extend the project by asking the user for a city name and displaying the weather for that city. Here's how you can do that:

```python
import requests

def get_weather(city):
    api_key = "your_api_key_here"
    url =
f"http://api.openweathermap.org/data/2.5/weather?q={c
ity}&appid={api_key}&units=metric"

    response = requests.get(url)

    if response.status_code == 200:
        data = response.json()
        temperature = data['main']['temp']
        weather_description =
data['weather'][0]['description']
```

```
        humidity = data['main']['humidity']
        wind_speed = data['wind']['speed']

        print(f"Weather in {city}:")
        print(f"Temperature: {temperature}°C")
        print(f"Description: {weather_description}")
        print(f"Humidity: {humidity}%")
        print(f"Wind Speed: {wind_speed} m/s")
    else:
        print(f"Failed to retrieve weather data.
Status code: {response.status_code}")

if __name__ == "__main__":
    city = input("Enter a city name: ")
    get_weather(city)
```

This program:

- Prompts the user to enter a city name.
- Fetches the weather data for that city and displays it to the user.

Best Practices for API Integration

When working with APIs, there are several best practices to keep in mind to ensure that your application is efficient, secure, and maintainable.

1. Handle API Errors Gracefully

Always check for errors when making requests to an API. Many things can go wrong, such as incorrect API keys, invalid parameters, or network issues. Always check the HTTP status code and handle errors appropriately.

```python
if response.status_code == 200:
```

```
    data = response.json()
    # process the data
else:
    print(f"Error: {response.status_code} -
{response.text}")
```

Common HTTP status codes:

- `200 OK`: Successful request.
- `400 Bad Request`: Invalid request (e.g., missing parameters).
- `401 Unauthorized`: Invalid API key or lack of authentication.
- `404 Not Found`: Resource not found (e.g., incorrect city name).
- `500 Internal Server Error`: Server-side error.

2. Limit API Calls and Use Caching

Many APIs have rate limits, meaning you can only make a certain number of requests per hour or day. To avoid hitting these limits, you should:

- Cache API responses to avoid making unnecessary requests.
- Use a tool like **Redis** or Python's built-in `cachetools` library to store responses for a short time.

3. Use Environment Variables for API Keys

For security reasons, never hardcode your API keys directly into your source code. Instead, store them in environment variables and access them securely at runtime.

```python
python

import os
api_key = os.getenv("API_KEY")
```

4. Validate User Input

When accepting user input, always validate it to avoid sending malformed requests to the API. For example, ensure that the city name is a valid string and handle cases where the input is empty or invalid.

```python
city = input("Enter a city name: ")
if not city:
    print("City name cannot be empty.")
else:
    get_weather(city)
```

5. Understand API Limits and Documentation

Before using an API, read its documentation thoroughly. Most APIs have rate limits, data formats, and usage guidelines that you should be aware of to avoid problems. Also, make sure you understand the correct parameters for making requests.

Conclusion

In this chapter, we learned about **APIs** (Application Programming Interfaces) and how they enable applications to communicate with each other. We explored the basics of using **Python's Requests library** to interact with APIs, covering GET and POST requests, handling responses, and making dynamic API calls.

Through the **Weather Forecast App** project, we built a simple application that fetches weather data from an API and displays it to the user. This hands-on experience helped solidify the concepts of working with APIs and using Python to interact with external services.

We also discussed best practices for API integration, such as handling errors, using environment variables for API keys, caching responses, and validating user input.

Chapter 14: Version Control with Git and GitHub

Introduction to Version Control

Version control is a system that helps track changes to files or sets of files over time. This system allows you to maintain a history of your work, making it easier to revert to previous versions, collaborate with others, and manage the evolution of a project. Version control is particularly important for software development, as it helps teams work together efficiently while avoiding conflicts and ensuring that each contributor's changes are properly tracked.

There are two main types of version control systems:

1. **Centralized Version Control**: In this system, there is a central repository, and every developer checks out a of the project from this central location. While this system has been widely used, it has limitations, such as the central server being a single point of failure.
2. **Distributed Version Control**: In this system, each developer has a full of the project, including its history. This enables greater flexibility and allows developers to work offline. **Git**, the most popular version control system today, is a distributed version control system.

In this chapter, we will focus on **Git**, a powerful and widely used version control system, and **GitHub**, a cloud-based service that hosts Git repositories. By the end of this chapter, you will have a solid understanding of how to use Git and GitHub to manage your projects, collaborate with others, and maintain an organized history of your work.

What is Version Control? Why Git?

What is Version Control?

Version control allows you to keep track of changes made to your files over time. Every time you make a change to a file and save it, version control systems like Git save that change in a history, so you can:

1. **Track Changes**: Version control keeps a record of all modifications, additions, and deletions made to a project. This allows you to see who made changes, when the changes were made, and why they were made.
2. **Collaborate with Others**: Version control makes it easy for multiple people to work on the same project without overwriting each other's changes. Changes can be made independently and merged together later.
3. **Revert to Previous Versions**: If something goes wrong, you can always go back to a previous state of your project. This helps you avoid losing work due to mistakes or issues introduced by new changes.
4. **Branching**: Version control allows you to work on separate "branches" of your project, making it easier to experiment or work on features without affecting the main project. Once the feature is ready, it can be merged back into the main branch.

Why Git?

Git is the most popular version control system used by developers worldwide. Here's why Git has become the go-to tool for version control:

1. **Distributed System**: Unlike centralized version control systems, Git allows each developer to have their own local of the entire repository, including its history. This makes it

easier to work offline, and allows developers to experiment without affecting the main project.

2. **Efficiency**: Git is fast and efficient, even with large projects. Its performance remains consistent, even as projects grow in size.
3. **Flexibility**: Git gives you full control over your project's history. You can create branches to work on new features, merge them back into the main project when they're ready, and even rewrite history if necessary.
4. **Collaboration**: Git enables smooth collaboration, allowing multiple developers to work on the same project without overwriting each other's work. Changes can be merged together, and Git helps handle any conflicts that arise.
5. **Open Source**: Git is free and open-source, with a huge community of developers constantly improving it.

Setting Up Git Locally and Remotely

To start using Git, you need to install it on your local machine and create an account on GitHub for remote hosting. Let's walk through the steps to get everything set up.

1. Installing Git Locally

To use Git on your computer, you first need to install it. Git is available for Windows, macOS, and Linux.

- **Windows**: Download the Git installer from https://git-scm.com/download/win and follow the installation instructions.
- **macOS**: Git can be installed via Homebrew by running `brew install git`. Alternatively, you can download the installer from the official Git website.
- **Linux**: On most Linux distributions, you can install Git using your package manager, for example:

```
bash

sudo apt install git  # On Debian-based systems
like Ubuntu
```

After installation, verify that Git is installed by running the following command in your terminal or command prompt:

```
bash

git --version
```

This should display the version of Git that you installed.

2. Setting Up Git Configuration

Once Git is installed, you need to configure your name and email address. This information will be used to identify you in commit history. Run the following commands to set your name and email:

```
bash

git config --global user.name "Your Name"
git config --global user.email
"youremail@example.com"
```

3. Setting Up GitHub Account

To work with Git repositories remotely, you need a **GitHub** account. GitHub is a platform that hosts Git repositories, allowing developers to collaborate on projects, track issues, and manage codebases. Here's how to get started:

1. Go to https://github.com and create a free account.
2. After signing up, you'll be able to create repositories, manage your projects, and collaborate with others.

4. Connecting Git to GitHub

To push your local repositories to GitHub, you need to authenticate Git with your GitHub account. The most secure way to do this is by using **SSH keys**. You can also use HTTPS, but SSH is recommended for security and convenience.

Here's how to set up SSH keys:

1. Generate an SSH key on your local machine using the following command (replace with your email):

   ```bash
   ssh-keygen -t rsa -b 4096 -C
   "youremail@example.com"
   ```

2. Press `Enter` to accept the default location for the SSH key.
3. After generating the key, add it to your GitHub account by ing the public key. Run:

   ```bash
   cat ~/.ssh/id_rsa.pub
   ```

   the output, and then go to your GitHub account:

   - In the GitHub UI, go to **Settings** → **SSH and GPG keys** → **New SSH key**.
   - Paste the copied key into the key field and save.

Now your local Git is connected to GitHub via SSH, allowing you to push code to remote repositories securely.

Committing Changes and Pushing to GitHub

Once you've set up Git locally and connected it to GitHub, you can start working with your project and making commits. Here's how to commit changes and push them to GitHub.

1. Creating a Git Repository

Start by initializing a Git repository in your project folder. Navigate to your project directory and run:

```bash
git init
```

This will create a `.git` folder in your project, which Git uses to track changes.

2. Tracking Changes

After initializing the repository, you can start tracking changes. First, check the status of your project:

```bash
git status
```

Git will show the files that have been modified or added.

3. Adding Files to Staging Area

Before committing changes, you need to add the modified files to the staging area. You can add specific files or add all changes at once:

```bash
git add .  # Adds all changes to the staging area
```

Or, if you want to add individual files:

bash

```
git add filename.py
```

4. Committing Changes

Once you've staged the files, you can commit the changes. A commit represents a snapshot of your project at a specific point in time.

bash

```
git commit -m "Your commit message here"
```

The -m flag allows you to include a message describing the changes in the commit. Writing meaningful commit messages is essential for tracking the history of your project.

5. Pushing Changes to GitHub

To upload your local commits to GitHub, you need to add a remote repository. This is the URL of your GitHub repository. To add the remote repository, run:

bash

```
git remote add origin
https://github.com/username/repository.git
```

Replace username/repository.git with your actual GitHub username and repository name.

Next, push your local commits to GitHub:

bash

```
git push -u origin master
```

This command pushes your commits to the `master` branch of your GitHub repository. The `-u` flag sets the default remote for future pushes.

Project: Collaborative Project Using Git and GitHub

Now, let's walk through a collaborative project using Git and GitHub. This will help you understand how Git and GitHub are used in real-world team scenarios.

1. Setting Up a Collaborative Project

In this project, we will work together with others on the same repository. The process involves:

- **Creating a GitHub repository** to store the project.
- **Cloning the repository** to work on it locally.
- **Collaborating** by making commits, pushing changes, and pulling updates from other team members.

Creating a GitHub Repository

Start by creating a new repository on GitHub. Go to your GitHub account and click the "New" button on the repositories page. Give the repository a name, and optionally initialize it with a README file.

Cloning the Repository

Once the repository is created, you can clone it to your local machine to start working on it:

bash

```
git clone https://github.com/username/repository.git
```

This command copies the entire repository (including its history) to your local machine.

Working on the Project

As a team, each developer works on their local of the project. You can make changes, commit them, and push them to the shared repository.

2. Handling Merge Conflicts

One of the challenges when working with Git in a team is **merge conflicts**. Merge conflicts occur when two developers make changes to the same part of a file. Git cannot automatically merge these changes and requires the developers to resolve the conflict manually.

Example of a Merge Conflict

Let's say Developer A changes line 10 of a file, and Developer B changes line 10 of the same file. When Developer A pushes their changes and Developer B tries to push theirs, Git will throw a conflict error.

To resolve the conflict:

1. Pull the latest changes from GitHub:

    bash

    ```
    git pull origin master
    ```

2. Git will mark the conflict in the file, and you will need to manually edit the file to resolve the conflict.
3. After resolving the conflict, add the file back to the staging area:

```bash
git add filename.py
```

4. Commit the changes:

```bash
git commit -m "Resolved merge conflict in filename.py"
```

5. Finally, push the resolved changes:

```bash
git push origin master
```

3. Branching and Merging

Git's branching feature allows each developer to work on a separate "branch" of the project. This way, they can develop features independently without interfering with the main project. Once the feature is complete, it can be merged back into the main branch.

Creating a New Branch

To create a new branch, use the following command:

```bash
git checkout -b feature-branch
```

This creates a new branch called `feature-branch` and switches to it.

Merging a Branch

Once your feature is complete, you can merge it back into the `master` branch:

1. Switch back to the `master` branch:

   bash

   ```
   git checkout master
   ```

2. Merge your feature branch:

   bash

   ```
   git merge feature-branch
   ```

3. Push the merged changes to GitHub:

   bash

   ```
   git push origin master
   ```

Best Practices for Database Interaction

1. Write Meaningful Commit Messages

A good commit message should explain **why** a change was made, not just **what** was changed. For example, instead of writing "Fixed bug", write "Fixed issue with login form validation".

2. Commit Frequently

Make small, frequent commits. This makes it easier to track changes and revert to previous versions if necessary.

3. Use Branches for Features and Fixes

When working on a new feature or bug fix, always create a new branch. This keeps the `master` branch clean and ensures that your work can be reviewed and merged when it's complete.

4. Pull Regularly

If you're working in a team, always **pull** the latest changes from the remote repository before you start working. This ensures that you're working with the most up-to-date version of the project.

bash

```
git pull origin master
```

5. Use .gitignore Files

To prevent unnecessary files (like logs, compiled code, or dependency files) from being committed to the repository, use a .gitignore file. This file lists patterns for files and directories that should be ignored by Git.

Conclusion

In this chapter, we explored **Git**, a powerful version control system that is essential for managing code and collaborating on projects. We covered the following key topics:

- **What version control is** and why Git is widely used in the software development world.
- **Setting up Git** on your local machine and connecting it to GitHub.
- **Committing changes**, **pushing to GitHub**, and working with remote repositories.
- **Collaborative project workflows**, including handling merge conflicts and branching.
- **Best practices** for version control to keep your code organized and maintainable.

By understanding and mastering Git and GitHub, you will be equipped to work effectively in team settings and maintain a clean, versioned history of your codebase.

Chapter 15: Landing Your First Tech Job: The Final Steps

Introduction

Securing your first job in the tech industry can be both an exciting and challenging journey. After spending months learning Python, mastering the fundamentals, and working on personal projects, you're now ready to take the final steps towards landing your dream job. But how do you stand out from the crowd? How do you showcase your skills in a way that grabs the attention of hiring managers and recruiters?

In this chapter, we'll explore the essential steps you need to take to increase your chances of landing your first tech job. We'll cover how to:

1. **Build your portfolio** to showcase your Python projects.
2. **Create an impressive resume** tailored for tech jobs.
3. **Prepare for technical interviews** to make a strong impression.
4. **Implement job search strategies** including networking and freelancing.
5. **Build a portfolio website** using **Python** and **Flask** to demonstrate your skills.

By the end of this chapter, you'll be ready to present yourself as a strong candidate for your first tech job and continue your journey as a Python developer.

Building Your Portfolio: Showcasing Your Python Projects

One of the most powerful tools you can use to land a tech job is a well-curated **portfolio**. A portfolio serves as a concrete representation of your skills, experience, and problem-solving ability. It demonstrates what you've worked on, how you approach challenges, and the tools you are familiar with. In the world of software development, your portfolio is often more important than your resume.

Why a Portfolio Matters

Hiring managers and recruiters want to see your work in action. A portfolio allows you to:

- **Showcase your coding skills**: Employers can review your code directly.
- **Demonstrate problem-solving abilities**: Highlight projects where you tackled specific challenges.
- **Exhibit your growth**: Show how your skills have developed over time by including a variety of projects.

What Should Be Included in Your Portfolio?

When building your portfolio, focus on quality over quantity. It's better to have a few well-thought-out, polished projects than a large number of unfinished or low-quality ones. Here are some key elements to include:

1. **Diverse Projects**: Include a mix of projects that showcase your range of skills. For example:
   o **Web applications** using Flask or Django.
   o **Data analysis** projects using pandas and NumPy.
   o **Automation scripts** to demonstrate your ability to solve real-world problems.

- o **APIs** that interact with external services.
2. **Well-Documented Code**: Your code should be clean, well-commented, and easy to understand. Add a README file to each project explaining:
    - o What the project does.
    - o How to run the project.
    - o The technologies used.
    - o Any challenges you faced and how you solved them.
3. **GitHub Repositories**: Every project should be hosted on GitHub, as this allows potential employers to review your code, track your progress, and see your commitment to version control.
4. **Live Demos**: If possible, host your projects online so that employers can see them in action. Platforms like **Heroku**, **Netlify**, and **GitHub Pages** offer free hosting for small projects. For web applications, this provides an opportunity for recruiters to interact with your project.
5. **Personal Projects**: Don't be afraid to include personal projects or projects done during your learning process. Personal projects show initiative and passion, which are highly valued by employers.
6. **Collaborative Projects**: If possible, include open-source or collaborative projects to showcase your ability to work in teams and use tools like Git for version control.

Organizing Your Portfolio

A portfolio website is the perfect way to showcase your projects and present yourself professionally. You can organize your portfolio into several key sections:

- **Home Page**: A brief introduction to who you are, your skills, and what you're passionate about.
- **Projects**: A gallery of your projects with descriptions and links to their GitHub repositories or live demos.
- **Blog (Optional)**: Share your learning experiences, tutorials, and insights on Python or software development.

- **Contact Information**: Make it easy for potential employers to reach out to you.

Creating an Impressive Resume for Tech Jobs

Your resume is often the first impression a recruiter or hiring manager will have of you. A strong, tailored resume is essential for landing interviews. Unlike resumes in other industries, tech resumes should focus more on **skills**, **projects**, and **experience** rather than just your education.

Key Elements of a Tech Resume

1. **Contact Information**: Include your name, phone number, email address, and links to your GitHub profile, LinkedIn, and portfolio website. Ensure your contact information is easy to find and up-to-date.
2. **Summary/Objective**: Write a brief summary at the top of your resume that highlights your key skills, experience, and what you're looking for. For example:
    - "Passionate Python developer with experience building web applications using Flask and Django. Seeking a software engineering role where I can contribute to impactful projects and continue growing my skills in data analysis and machine learning."
3. **Skills**: List your technical skills, including programming languages, frameworks, tools, and technologies. For example:
    - **Languages**: Python, JavaScript, HTML/CSS
    - **Frameworks**: Flask, Django, React
    - **Libraries**: pandas, NumPy, Matplotlib
    - **Tools**: Git, Docker, Jenkins
4. **Projects**: Highlight key projects in your portfolio that are relevant to the job you're applying for. Be sure to describe the

technologies used, your role in the project, and the outcomes or impact of the project. For example:

- o **Weather Forecast App**: Built a Flask-based web app that fetches weather data from an external API and displays it in a user-friendly interface. Used Python, Flask, and the OpenWeather API.

5. **Experience**: If you have relevant work experience, list it here. For junior developers, this might include internships, freelance work, or part-time roles. Focus on the skills you gained and the projects you contributed to.

6. **Education**: If you have a degree in computer science, software engineering, or a related field, include it here. If you've taken any online courses or bootcamps, list those as well. For example:

- o **Bachelor of Science in Computer Science –** University of XYZ
- o **Python for Data Science (Coursera)** – 2022

7. **Certifications**: Include any relevant certifications, such as those for Python, machine learning, or web development.

Formatting Your Resume

A clean, well-organized resume is easier for hiring managers to read. Here are a few tips:

- **Keep it concise**: Limit your resume to one page if you have less than 5 years of experience. For more experienced developers, two pages may be appropriate.
- **Use bullet points**: This makes your resume easier to scan.
- **Avoid jargon**: Keep your language simple and clear.
- **Highlight achievements**: Focus on what you've accomplished rather than just listing tasks.
- **Tailor your resume**: Customize your resume for each job application. Highlight the skills and experience that are most relevant to the specific role.

Preparing for Technical Interviews

The technical interview is the most challenging part of the hiring process for many developers. It tests your problem-solving abilities, coding skills, and how you think under pressure. Here's how to prepare effectively.

1. Understand the Basics

Make sure you have a solid understanding of Python fundamentals, including:

- **Data types** (strings, lists, dictionaries, sets, etc.)
- **Control flow** (if/else statements, loops)
- **Functions** and **methods**
- **Classes** and **object-oriented programming**
- **File handling** (reading/writing files)
- **Error handling** (try/except)

2. Practice Coding Problems

Technical interviews often involve coding challenges that test your problem-solving abilities. Websites like **LeetCode**, **HackerRank**, and **CodeSignal** provide a wealth of coding problems to practice. Here are some tips:

- **Start with easy problems**: Build your confidence by solving basic problems first.
- **Move to medium/hard problems**: Once you're comfortable, tackle more difficult problems to improve your skills.
- **Practice algorithm and data structure questions**: Many technical interviews focus on common algorithms (sorting, searching) and data structures (arrays, linked lists, trees).

3. Explain Your Thought Process

During the interview, it's important to explain your thought process as you solve the problem. Don't just write code silently. Talk through your approach and explain your reasoning behind each decision. This demonstrates your problem-solving skills and how you approach challenges.

4. Learn System Design

System design interviews assess your ability to design scalable and efficient systems. Learn the fundamentals of system design, such as load balancing, caching, database design, and microservices architecture. Resources like **Grokking the System Design Interview** can help you prepare.

5. Mock Interviews

Simulate real interview conditions by practicing with mock interviews. This will help you get comfortable with the interview process and receive constructive feedback. Websites like **Pramp** and **Interviewing.io** offer free mock interview platforms.

Job Search Strategies: Networking and Freelancing

Job hunting in the tech industry can be a competitive process. To stand out, you need a combination of **networking, freelancing**, and **targeted job search strategies**.

1. Networking

Building a professional network is one of the most effective ways to find job opportunities. Here's how to do it:

- **LinkedIn**: Create a professional LinkedIn profile and connect with people in your field. Share relevant content, engage with others, and reach out to people in your network for advice or job opportunities.
- **Meetups**: Attend local or virtual tech meetups, hackathons, and conferences to connect with other developers and companies.
- **GitHub**: Contribute to open-source projects on GitHub. This helps you build your portfolio and get noticed by potential employers.
- **Referrals**: Many companies hire through referrals, so let your network know you're job hunting. Reaching out to former colleagues or classmates can lead to valuable opportunities.

2. Freelancing

Freelancing can be a great way to gain experience, build your portfolio, and generate income while you search for a full-time job. Platforms like **Upwork, Fiverr**, and **Freelancer** allow you to find projects that match your skills.

- **Start small**: Take on smaller projects initially to build your reputation.
- **Leverage your portfolio**: Use your portfolio website and GitHub to showcase your previous work.
- **Communicate effectively**: Clear communication with clients is key to building strong relationships and getting repeat work.

3. Targeted Job Search

Use job boards like **Indeed, Glassdoor**, and **LinkedIn** to search for job openings. Tailor your resume and cover letter for each position, highlighting the skills and experience that match the job description. Don't forget to leverage your network for referrals and introductions.

Project: Build Your Portfolio Website Using Python and Flask

Building a portfolio website is a great way to showcase your projects, skills, and experience. In this project, we'll build a simple portfolio website using **Flask**, a lightweight Python web framework.

Step 1: Set Up Your Flask Application

First, create a new directory for your portfolio project and set up a virtual environment:

bash

```
mkdir portfolio
cd portfolio
python -m venv venv
source venv/bin/activate  # On macOS/Linux
venv\Scripts\activate  # On Windows
```

Install Flask:

bash

```
pip install Flask
```

Create a file called `app.py` to define your Flask application:

python

```
from flask import Flask, render_template

app = Flask(__name__)

@app.route('/')
def home():
    return render_template('index.html')

if __name__ == '__main__':
    app.run(debug=True)
```

Step 2: Create HTML Templates

Inside your project directory, create a `templates` folder. In this folder, create an `index.html` file to serve as the homepage of your portfolio:

html

```
<!DOCTYPE html>
<html lang="en">
<head>
    <meta charset="UTF-8">
    <meta name="viewport" content="width=device-
width, initial-scale=1.0">
    <title>My Portfolio</title>
</head>
<body>
    <h1>Welcome to My Portfolio</h1>
    <p>This is where I showcase my projects and
skills.</p>
</body>
</html>
```

Step 3: Add More Pages

You can add more pages to your portfolio, such as a "Projects" page, "About Me" section, or "Contact" form. Create additional HTML templates for these pages and define routes in your `app.py` to render them.

Step 4: Deploying Your Portfolio

Once you've created your portfolio, deploy it online using a platform like **Heroku** or **Netlify**. Follow the deployment instructions for your chosen platform to get your site live.

Conclusion: Continuing Your Python Journey and Next Steps

Landing your first tech job is just the beginning of your career as a Python developer. As you continue your journey, keep improving your skills, building new projects, and staying up-to-date with the latest technologies. Here are some next steps to consider:

1. **Build a Personal Brand**: Write blogs, contribute to open-source projects, and share your knowledge with the developer community.
2. **Learn New Frameworks**: Dive deeper into web development with Django, explore data science with libraries like **TensorFlow**, or learn about cloud computing.
3. **Stay Curious**: The tech industry is always evolving. Stay curious, learn new tools and technologies, and continuously improve your skills.
4. **Get Certified**: Consider pursuing certifications in specialized areas, such as **machine learning**, **cloud computing**, or **data engineering**.

With persistence, hard work, and a strong portfolio, you will be well on your way to success in the tech industry. Keep learning, stay focused, and enjoy the journey!

Additional Resources

As a Python developer, continuous learning and staying up-to-date with the latest tools, trends, and challenges are essential to growing and succeeding in your career. This section provides a variety of resources that can help you strengthen your Python skills and stay engaged with the broader Python community. Whether you're looking for a quick reference, discovering new tools, or joining Python-related challenges and competitions, these resources will guide you along your journey.

Appendix A: Python Cheat Sheet

A **cheat sheet** is an invaluable tool for developers, offering quick access to key syntax and concepts. It acts as a reference guide that can save time when you're coding, ensuring that you can quickly look up functions, methods, or features you're less familiar with. Below is an expanded cheat sheet that covers some of the most commonly used Python features and syntax.

1. Basic Syntax

- **Print Statement**: Output text or variables to the console.

  ```python
  print("Hello, World!")
  ```

- **Variables**: Assign values to variables.

  ```python
  x = 10
  y = 5
  result = x + y
  ```

```
print(result)
```

2. Data Types

- **Integer**: Whole numbers.

  python

  ```
  age = 25
  ```

- **Float**: Decimal numbers.

  python

  ```
  pi = 3.14159
  ```

- **String**: Text data enclosed in quotes.

  python

  ```
  name = "Alice"
  ```

- **List**: Ordered collection of items.

  python

  ```
  fruits = ["apple", "banana", "cherry"]
  ```

- **Dictionary**: Unordered collection of key-value pairs.

  python

  ```
  person = {"name": "John", "age": 30}
  ```

- **Tuple**: Immutable ordered collection of items.

  python

  ```
  coordinates = (4, 5)
  ```

3. Control Flow

- **If-Else Statements**: Conditional statements to execute based on conditions.

python

```python
if age >= 18:
    print("Adult")
else:
    print("Minor")
```

- **For Loop**: Iterates over a sequence (e.g., list, tuple, string).

python

```python
for fruit in fruits:
    print(fruit)
```

- **While Loop**: Executes as long as the condition is true.

python

```python
i = 0
while i < 5:
    print(i)
    i += 1
```

4. Functions

- **Defining a Function**: Functions allow you to group code into reusable blocks.

python

```python
def greet(name):
    return f"Hello, {name}!"
```

- **Function Call**: Invoke a function to execute it.

```python
```

```python
message = greet("Alice")
print(message)
```

5. Modules and Libraries

- **Importing a Module**: Use external modules or libraries to extend Python's capabilities.

```python
```

```python
import math
print(math.sqrt(16))   # Output: 4.0
```

- **Import Specific Functions**: You can import specific functions from a module to avoid using the full module name.

```python
```

```python
from math import pi
print(pi)   # Output: 3.14159
```

6. File Handling

- **Opening a File**: Use open() to access files.

```python
```

```python
file = open('example.txt', 'r')
content = file.read()
print(content)
file.close()
```

- **Writing to a File**: Use the write mode ('w') to write to a file.

```python
```

```python
with open('output.txt', 'w') as file:
    file.write("Hello, File!")
```

Appendix B: Recommended Python Tools and Editors

The right tools and editors can significantly improve your productivity as a Python developer. Below are some of the most popular and recommended tools and editors that every Python developer should consider using.

1. Integrated Development Environments (IDEs)

IDEs provide powerful features such as code completion, debugging, and syntax highlighting. Here are some of the top IDEs for Python development:

- **PyCharm**: One of the most popular Python IDEs, PyCharm provides excellent code navigation, a built-in debugger, testing support, and integration with Git. It is available in both a free community edition and a paid professional edition.
- **VS Code (Visual Studio Code)**: A lightweight yet powerful text editor by Microsoft. With the Python extension, it provides features such as syntax highlighting, linting, IntelliSense (auto-completion), debugging, and integrated Git support.
- **Spyder**: A popular IDE for scientific computing and data science, Spyder integrates well with libraries such as NumPy, pandas, and Matplotlib. It comes with powerful tools like an interactive console and variable explorer.
- **Jupyter Notebooks**: Ideal for data scientists and analysts, Jupyter allows you to combine code, output, and rich text in a single document. It's commonly used for data analysis, machine learning, and visualization.

2. Code Editors

If you prefer lighter, more customizable code editors, here are some options:

- **Sublime Text**: A fast, cross-platform text editor with features like multi-caret editing, a powerful search, and a variety of plugins to enhance your development workflow.
- **Atom**: An open-source text editor with a strong community and support for various packages that can be installed to add functionality like syntax highlighting, linters, and version control.
- **Vim**: A powerful, keyboard-centric text editor. It has a steeper learning curve but is highly customizable and extremely efficient once mastered.

3. Version Control and Collaboration Tools

Version control is essential for managing changes to your code and collaborating with others.

- **Git**: A distributed version control system that allows you to track changes, collaborate on code, and manage your project's history.
- **GitHub**: A platform that hosts your Git repositories and provides tools for collaborating with others, such as issue tracking, pull requests, and code reviews.
- **GitLab**: An alternative to GitHub, GitLab also offers Git repository hosting and CI/CD integration, and it's a great tool for teams.

4. Virtual Environments

Virtual environments are essential for managing dependencies in Python projects. They allow you to create isolated environments for each project, avoiding conflicts between packages.

- **venv**: The built-in tool for creating virtual environments in Python. It's simple to use and is included with Python by default.
- **Conda**: A package and environment manager that is especially useful for data science projects. Conda handles dependencies and environments, and it integrates well with popular libraries like NumPy and pandas.
- **Pipenv**: A tool that automatically creates and manages a virtual environment for your Python projects and adds/removes packages from your `Pipfile` as you install/uninstall packages.

Appendix C: Python Challenges and Competitions to Join

Getting involved in coding challenges and competitions is a great way to improve your problem-solving skills, learn new techniques, and meet other developers. Here are some of the top platforms and competitions you should consider joining:

1. LeetCode

LeetCode is an online platform that offers coding challenges to help you prepare for technical interviews. The challenges range in difficulty from easy to hard, and they cover algorithms, data structures, databases, and more. LeetCode also offers a premium subscription with additional features.

- **Why LeetCode?**: Excellent for practicing coding problems that are common in technical interviews. It also has a large community where you can discuss solutions and techniques.

2. HackerRank

HackerRank is another popular platform for practicing coding problems, but it also offers challenges in algorithms, mathematics, SQL, and even interview preparation. HackerRank's practice problems are categorized by difficulty and topic, making it easier to find relevant challenges.

- **Why HackerRank?**: Great for beginners and intermediate developers. HackerRank also hosts coding competitions and hackathons, offering the chance to win prizes and connect with other developers.

3. Codewars

Codewars offers a wide range of coding challenges, or "kata," that allow you to practice and improve your coding skills. The platform's unique feature is that the challenges are ranked by difficulty, so you can progress at your own pace.

- **Why Codewars?**: It provides an interactive and community-driven learning environment. You can see how others solve the same problems and learn from their approaches.

4. TopCoder

TopCoder is one of the oldest competitive programming platforms and hosts competitions in algorithms, data science, and design. It's known for hosting competitive programming contests that draw global participation.

- **Why TopCoder?**: It provides a chance to compete at a high level and can lead to job opportunities with major tech companies.

5. Google Code Jam

Google Code Jam is an annual competition where developers around the world compete in solving algorithmic problems. It's known for its challenging problems and attracts top programmers globally.

- **Why Google Code Jam?**: Competing in Google's Code Jam is a fantastic way to demonstrate your problem-solving abilities. It's also a prestigious competition with great rewards.

6. Project Euler

Project Euler is a platform that challenges you to solve mathematical and computational problems using programming. It's ideal for those who enjoy applying Python to solve complex problems with a mathematical foundation.

- **Why Project Euler?**: It's a fun and challenging way to apply your Python skills in the realms of mathematics and problem-solving.

7. Kaggle

For those interested in **data science** and **machine learning**, Kaggle is the go-to platform. Kaggle hosts competitions that involve real-world datasets and often challenge participants to build predictive models. It's an excellent platform for anyone looking to make a mark in the data science community.

- **Why Kaggle?**: Kaggle competitions provide real-world challenges that allow you to apply Python and data science skills in a competitive setting.

Appendix D: How to Stay Up-to-Date with Python Trends

Python is constantly evolving, with new features, libraries, and tools being released regularly. Staying up-to-date with the latest trends is crucial for remaining competitive in the tech industry. Here are some strategies to keep your Python knowledge current:

1. Follow Python Blogs

Many experienced Python developers and companies publish regular blogs that cover new features, tutorials, and best practices. Some popular Python blogs to follow include:

- **Real Python**: Offers in-depth tutorials and articles on all aspects of Python programming.
- **Python Software Foundation Blog**: Official blog of the Python Software Foundation, covering Python-related news and events.
- **PyBites**: A blog dedicated to Python coding challenges, tutorials, and tips.

2. Subscribe to Python Newsletters

Newsletters provide a great way to stay updated with the latest trends, tools, and libraries in Python. Consider subscribing to:

- **Python Weekly**: A weekly newsletter with the latest Python news, articles, and tutorials.
- **PyCoder's Weekly**: A curated newsletter that features tutorials, news, and resources for Python developers.

3. Attend Python Conferences and Meetups

Python conferences like **PyCon, DjangoCon**, and **SciPy** are great opportunities to learn about the latest trends in Python development, network with other developers, and attend workshops.

- **PyCon**: The largest annual Python conference, where developers from around the world gather to share their knowledge.
- **DjangoCon**: A conference specifically for Django developers, focusing on best practices, new features, and community discussions.
- **Meetups**: Search for local Python meetups in your area or attend virtual meetups. Websites like **Meetup.com** offer Python-focused events for networking and learning.

4. Follow Influential Python Developers

Many experienced Python developers share their insights on Twitter, blogs, and YouTube. Some influential Python figures to follow include:

- **Guido van Rossum** (Creator of Python)
- **Raymond Hettinger** (Core Python Developer)
- **Kenneth Reitz** (Creator of `requests`)

5. Stay Active on Python Forums

Engage in Python communities like **Stack Overflow, Reddit** (r/learnpython, r/Python), and **Python Discord**. These forums provide valuable advice, allow you to ask questions, and keep you informed about the latest developments in Python.

Conclusion

In this chapter, we've explored a wealth of resources to help you succeed as a Python developer. From building a portfolio and crafting an impressive resume to preparing for technical interviews and engaging in coding competitions, the resources provided will give you the edge you need to land your first job in tech.

By staying up-to-date with Python trends, participating in coding challenges, and leveraging the best tools and resources, you can continue to develop your skills and advance your career. Keep learning, stay engaged with the Python community, and never stop building—your journey as a Python developer is just beginning!